Charles Warren Currier

Dimitrios and Irene

or, The conquest of Constantinople, a historical romance

Charles Warren Currier

Dimitrios and Irene
or, The conquest of Constantinople, a historical romance

ISBN/EAN: 9783742861177

Manufactured in Europe, USA, Canada, Australia, Japa

Cover: Foto ©ninafisch / pixelio.de

Manufactured and distributed by brebook publishing software (www.brebook.com)

Charles Warren Currier

Dimitrios and Irene

PREFACE.

Not long since, my interest became centered in that sanguinary revolution which, in the beginning of our age, gave back to the Greeks the independence of which they had so long been deprived. The occasion of this was a small but most interesting story sent to me by its author, my distinguished friend, M. Dimitrios Bikelas, of Athens. *Louki Laras* awakened within me a desire to continue the study of the same subject. My mind became riveted on the Turks, who, in this century, as of old, have displayed such ferocious barbarity, for instance, in the massacre of Scio.—From the present, my thoughts reverted to the past, I contemplated the fall of Byzantium, and the story I now offer to the reader has been the outcome.

I did not know when I began this tale that the distinguished author of "Ben Hur" had prepared a Historical Romance the scene of which is laid in the same place and time as my own. However, though in the great historical outlines resembling each other, they are worked out on plans essentially different. May the little work I now send forth to the world serve to increase the interest of the public in a most interesting epoch of history! It seems to me a favorable coincidence that it should appear at a time, when there is a marked tendency toward a union between the Eastern and Western churches, a tendency upon which especial stress is laid by an Encyclical of the Holy Father which is announced for the near future.

THE AUTHOR.

DIMITRIOS AND IRENE;
OR,
THE CONQUEST OF CONSTANTINOPLE.

CHAPTER I.

It was towards the end of March, 1453. The day was drawing to a close, and the last rays of the sun as it descended ever lower toward the western horizon, cast a mellow reflection on the dome of St. Sophia, the patriarchal church of Constantinople, in which city our story begins. On a stone step at one of the doors of this venerable pile, erected by the piety of the Emperor Justinian, sat an aged priest whose furrowed brow, long white locks and flowing beard which descended to his breast, gave him the appearance of one of the prophets of old. At least sixty years seemed to have passed over his head. He was attired in a long black robe, girded at the waist, with wide sleeves, and on his head he wore a hood like that of the monks, while the cape around his shoulders was adorned with a number of crosses. From under this cape, a black mantle descended to his feet, which were covered with sandals. Any one acquainted with oriental monasticism, would at once have recognized a monk of the Order of St. Basil, clad in the great or angelical habit. Beside the aged man sat a youth of twenty summers. His curly locks descended to his shoulders, his face slightly bronzed, was of the rue Grecian type, and it bore an expression of thoughtfulness and even marks of anxiety. He wore a loose white tunic reaching to his knees, while a species of mantle was carelessly hung over his shoulders. The two appeared to have been for sometime in earnest conversation, which had been followed by silence that lasted a few minutes. The first to interrupt it was the aged monk. As he spoke, there was something sad, yet sweet in his accents. A voice of deep tone contrasted well with the melody of the Attic dialect.

"It is true, Dimitrios, alas! too true, our proud city, our last stronghold, the only remnant of the glorious Roman Empire, the mistress of the world will soon be a slave of the Turk, Byzantium will be a thing of the past. O! that I should live to witness this day! Why do I not sleep with my fathers? In the grave at least the Turk wields no power."

"But, my father," replied the young man, "are things then so far gone? Is there no hope?"

"None, my child. You are aware of the fact that the Byzantine Empire has fallen piecemeal under the sway of the Turks. Since more than a century, the Empire of Constantine has been reduced to the small territory occupied by this city and a few provinces in the south. Ever since Prince Solyman crossed the Hellespont in the early part of the last century, the Turks have been encroaching upon us. Amurath I. subdued without resistance the whole province of Thrace from the Hellespont to Mount Hæmus and, since then, the standard of the Ottomans floats proudly from the walls of Adrianople. Bajazet I., the son of Amurath, continued the work of his father, extending his conquests over Thrace, Macedonia and Thessaly. Forgive this weakness, my son, but my blood boils within me when the image of a traitor arises before my eyes. Who delivered our beautiful, but sadly afflicted Greece into the hands of the infidel, who led Bajazet through the pass of Thermopylae, once in olden times defended by Leonidas and his heroic band, who? alas! my son, one of our own, another Judas, a successor of the Apostles, a Bishop of our holy church. Betrayed into the hands of the enemy by a minister of Christ! The provinces of Greece were overrun. The powerful Christian army, 100,000 strong, led by Sigismond, King of Hungary, was entirely conquered by the Mussulman, and, had the formidable invader not fallen into the hands of one greater than himself, the Tartar Tamerlane, the fate of Constantinople would probably have been sealed long ere this. The accession of Mahomet I. to the throne was a star of hope for our empire, but it was a star that shone only a short time in the firmament of history. His successor, Amurath II., would have laid siege to Constantinople, had an insurrection at Nice not turned aside his attention. When his mind reverted to our fair city, nothing saved it but the payment of the annual tribute of 300,000 aspers and the relinquishing of Thessalonica. You know the fate of that unfortunate city, how, after a desperate resistance it was overpowered by the Turks. Its riches were carried off, the churches, with one exception, turned into Mosques and the inhabitants led into captivity. Our day had not yet arrived, but, believe me, my son, it is not far distant. The heroism of the intrepid Scanderbeg in Albania kept the Turkish army occupied in another direction, but Scanderbeg is no more and Albania is in the power of the infidel. Mahomet II. now rules over the Ottoman Empire and we know not what day we may expect his hosts before the walls of Constantinople. I was in my monastery of Agios-Kyriani, when Athens fell into the hands of the Sultan, and, alas! it was our Hegumenos who carried to him the keys of the city. For that reason the tribute imposed on us by the conqueror is a small one."

Here the speaker interrupted his discourse as though overcome by some painful memory, and a tear glistened in his eye. Dimitrios, seeing that the monk was silent, thus began:

"The picture you have drawn is indeed most appalling, but may we not hope that, if Constantinople falls, at least, the lives of its inhabitants will be spared? At Thessalonica there was little bloodshed."

"True, my son, but a worse fate awaits our poor people. Slavery in its bitterest forms stares us in the face. Our men will serve the Turk, our children will be educated in the religion of the Prophet, our women will become the victims of brutal lust and fill the harems of the Sultan and his officers."

Here the young man covered his face with his hands, and, in a low voice, moaned: "Irene, my poor Irene, rather would I see thee in thy grave."

The monk noticed his emotion, and in a comforting tone, addressed him: "It is true, dreadful calamities hang over us, but remember there is a God; let us place our trust in Him." At this moment the shadow of a man was seen to glide before them; both the monk and Dimitrios raised their eyes and an individual disappeared around the corner of the sacred edifice. A deathlike pallor overspread the countenance of Dimitrios and a shudder passed over his frame, but in an instant he had regained his composure. His companion had not noticed his emotion, and, arising, said: "Dimitrios, the hour is advanced and I must leave you. To-morrow I leave Constantinople and return home, but I hope that we shall meet again under more joyful circumstances." Hereupon the monk and the young man embraced each other, the former entering the church and the latter pursuing his way along the street which passed between St. Sophia and the Hippodrome. He had not proceeded far when he heard his name called. Turning, he beheld the mysterous individual, the sight of whom had, a short time before, caused him to turn pale. Dimitrios, with teeth firmly set and knitted brows, awaited his arrival, while the other approached him, smiling. "Hail, Dimitrios," he exclaimed, "I saw thee sitting on the steps of St. Sophia, but dared not interrupt thy earnest conversation. Whither goest thou?"

"Hast thou aught to communicate to me?" replied Dimitrios.

"No! but I fain would keep thee company on thy way."

"I prefer to be alone."

"Come, come, Dimitrios, why look at me like a bear? I have done thee no harm."

"Thou hast done me no harm? Is it then no harm to come between me and my bethrothed, to use all means in thy power, vile insinuations, detestable and false accusations, heinous calumnies to separate her from me and win her for thyself whom she detests?"

Here a significant frown overshadowed the brow of the stranger whom we shall henceforth know as Nicolaus, while an ironical smile played upon his lips.

"Thou hast been misinformed, Dimitrios," he replied,

"thou hast no better friend in Constantinople than myself. I take Irene from thee! rather let my right hand wither. False friends have blackend me before thy eyes."

"Surely, Irene's father is not a false friend."

Nicolaus grew pale, but hiding his emotion, he answered: "Have I said aught to Irene's father concerning thee?"

"No! but thou did'st speak to others in order that thy insidious words should reach his ears."

"False, false; it is a lie."

"Moreover, Nicolaus, actions sometimes speak louder than words. A winking of the eye, a shrug of the shoulder may hurt a man's reputation as much as open calumny. I know how thou hast acted in the presence of Irene and her father."

"Dimitrios, I have been misunderstood. If I have innocently been the cause that the least injury has been done thee, I will endeavor to make amends. Give me thy hand, let us part as friends."

Dimitrios, though with evident aversion, extended his hand, which was heartily pressed by Nicolaus, and the two separated, the former taking a side street and Dimitrios pursuing his way. When Nicolaus found himself alone, his hand clutched convulsively at some object concealed under his cloak. For a moment he seemed to reflect, then muttered between his teeth: "Patience, Nicolaus, patience! The moment has not yet arrived. Revenge is sweet, but it becomes sweeter the more it is delayed. No! strike not yet, let a more horrible fate overtake him. Thy enemy shall fall. Irene shall yet be thine."

CHAPTER II.

For more than an hour the city had been wrapped in the shades of evening. In one of the rooms of a large house, overlooking that part of the harbor called the "Golden Horn," sat a small family, absorbed in the society of one another. The walls of the apartment were covered with the most exquisite Carrara marble, the polished surface of which reflected the glare of numerous torches, fixed in sockets projecting out of the walls. The ceiling was literally covered with plates of gold, worked most artistically, and representing various species of fruits and flowers. On the Mosaic floor were seen the figures of men on horseback, clad in the armor of Mediæval times, and wielding the spear. The apartment was divided from the inner ones by a row of Byzantine pillars, on which a costly tapestry, woven with silken thread, was suspended. The entrance to the house was an arched doorway, constructed in the style of Byzantium. Everything indicated opulence and refinement.

On a chair of cedar wood, partly gilded, sat a man whose appearance indicated that he was past the middle age of life. His furrowed brow, and the deep lines of his face showed that he had not gone through life without care. His eyes, deep in his head, sparkled with vivacity as he spoke, while the expression of his mouth denoted great firmness. John Diogenes was one of the few Greeks who had retained their wealth. On a low stool, at his feet, sat a maiden of seventeen, with her hand resting on his knee, while her face turned upward, showed a pair of black eyes, intently fixed upon her father. She was of surpassing beauty. Her raven hair, gracefully bound in a knot at the back of her head, left entirely exposed a forehead as white as portions of the marble on the wall. Her lips were slightly parted, exposing to view a row of teeth that looked like pearls, while on her cheeks bloomed the roses of youth and health. Her arms were bare from the shoulders down, while a loose, white robe enveloped her form. In front of the father knelt a boy of twelve, whose face bore a striking resemblance to his sister. His hands rested upon an illustrated book upon his father's knees, and his countenance denoted rapturous attention.

"Basil," spoke the father, "can you repeat to me, in a few words, what I told you last evening concerning the early history of our city?"

"Yes, father, I think I can. Byzantium was first settled in the sixth century before Christ, by Dorian Greeks, natives of the seaport town of Megara. With the exception of thirty years, during which it was held by the Persians, Byzantium maintained for three centuries its independence, although it was twice conquered by the Athenians, who, nevertheless, did not deprive it of its freedom. In the fourth century, the city fell under the power of Alexander, the Great, but after the death of Lysimachus, one of his successors, it was again free for a hundred years until it was absorbed by the great Roman Republic."

"It is well, my son, I am glad to see that your memory renders you such good service."

"Father, dear," chimed in Irene, "tell Basil how the

name of Byzantium was changed for that of Constantinople."

"Yes, father, do," spoke the boy, "give me another opportunity to practise my memory."

"With pleasure, my children. The history of the great Constantine is known to you, Irene, and you, Basil, are familiar with his name. Beholding himself at the head of the greatest empire the world has ever known, this able general and no less able administrator understood how necessary it was to protect the empire against the incursions of the barbarians. The danger arose from two quârters; from the Goths in the North, and from the Persians in the East. Moreover, the empire stretched over a great portion of Europe and Asia, and Constantine deemed it necessary that his capital should occupy a central position in the Empire, as well for the sake of greater facilities in holding the reins of government, as of having a watchful eye on the enemy. Rome, the ancient capital, more than half way down the Italian Peninsula, was most inconveniently located, and no city in the East offered such inducements as Byzantium, hence, the first Christian Emperor determined to transfer the seat of the empire to this city, to which he gave the name of "New Rome," but the people spontaneously called it Constantinople, and that name it has retained to the present day, it being still governed by the successors of its founder."

"Thank you, father!" exclaimed brother and sister in one accord. Basil continued: "Is our present reigning emperor, Constantine, a descendant of Constantine the Great?"

"No, my son, Constantine belongs to the house of Paleologos. He is a descendant of Michael VIII., an unprincipled general of the empire, who, about the year 1260, obtained the crown by intrigue, and supplanted the boy-emperor, John Ducas."

"But why did not the descendants of Constantine continue to reign over the Empire?"

"For the simple reason, child, that there were no descendants of Constantine left. The last was the Empress Pulcheria, sister of the Emperor Toeodosius II. She died childless about the year 457. Thus, you see, it is a long time since the race of Constantine has become extinct."

"They say, father," put in Irene, "that our present emperor is not a good man, because he has submitted to the Bishop of Rome."

"Our sovereign, my daughter, may be called the best prince the house of Paleologos has ever had, but, unfortunately, in one respect, he seems to be blinded. Following the example of John VI., his brother and predecessor, who submitted to the Latin Church, at Florence, a few years ago, in 1439, Constantine holds with Rome and the Roman Bishop."

"I do not know much concerning the difference between ourselves and the Latin Christians, father," said Basil.

"It is a long story, my son. Suffice it to say that the encroachments of the Bishop of Rome on the rights of the œcumenical Patriarchs grew to be so unendurable, and their assumption of authority so intolerable, that a breach occurred between the Eastern and Western Churches, under the patriarch Photius, which became final under Michael Cerularius. Moreover, the Latins are heretical in some of their opinions concerning the

Blessed Trinity, matters which are altogether above your comprehension."

"But why did John Paleologos return to the jurisdiction of the See of Rome, father?" asked Irene.

"He no doubt expected that the Pope would help him against the Turks, but that hope is vain."

"You make me tremble, father," said the boy, "when you mention that terrible name; is it true that the Turks are so near to our city?"

"Yes, my boy," said the father, with constrained indifference; "they have erected forts only a few miles away from Constantinople, at the narrowest point on the Bosphorus. A great train of cannon has been collected at Adrianople, and a powerful fleet of war galleys has been built in various ports of Asia."

"But, surely," said Basil, "our emperor and his soldiers will resist."

"What can the emperor do? The glory of the empire has waned and the war-like spirit that animated the Roman legions no longer exists. Moreover, the emperor has no more than four thousand troops at his command, and most of these are foreigners."

"But, will not the other nations of Christendom help us?" queried Irene; "the cause is a general one."

"The emperor," replied the father, "has exhausted his efforts in making appeals to the Pope and the Italian naval powers, but with what success? Nicholas V. has sent some money, and a few hundred Italian hirelings. Giovanni Giustiniani has brought us from Genoa no more than two galleys and three hundred men. From Venice we have received only a few soldiers. Thus it is useless to speak of resistance, we can rely only on God."

"But," exclaimed Basil, with energy, "what are the

Franks doing? Did they not send powerful armies for the deliverance of the holy places, and shall they now remain inactive?" After a moment's silence, when each one seemed to reflect, Basil added the question: "Father, who are the present rulers of Christendom ?"

"Nicholas V.," Diogenes answered, "is Pope, and he rules over Rome and the adjacent territory. The Italian Peninsula is divided into a number of smaller states, the republics in the northern and central portion of the Peninsula being too numerous to be spoken of in detail. Florence is practically governed by Cosmo de Medici, the family of Sforza rules at Milan, Francisco Foscari is doge at Venice, and the house of Arragon reigns over the kingdom of Naples. The Spanish Peninsula is divided into various states. Castile is now ruled by King John II., Queen Blanche and John I. are sovereigns of Navarra, Arragon has as king Ferdinand I. The southeastern portion of the peninsula is comprised in the Moorish kingdom of Granada. Frederick III. is the Emperor of the West, or rather, of the Germanic nations, Charles VII. is king of France, and in England reigns Henry VI. Thus, my son, you now behold in whose hands the destiny of the world reposes. The weakest of all is our own Emperor Constantine. From the West we need await no help."

"Hark! father," exclaimed Irene, "do you hear those distant sounds? What can they mean?"

John Diogenes listened, then spoke slowly: "Yes, I hear an unusual noise, but be not alarmed, for, in these troublous times, everything is apt to frighten one."

Meanwhile, the sounds drew nearer, human voices, and even the name of the Emperor might be distinguished above the din. At that moment, the door burst open, and a young man with signs of dismay upon his countenance, rushed in. Irene turned with a frightened look and exclaimed:

"Heavens! Dimitrios, what has happened? Are the Turks before the walls?"

"No, Irene," he replied, scarcely noticing the presence of her father, "I will tell you all, as soon as I shall have regained my composure."

Turning to the master of the house, he bowed, to him, saying: "Pardon me, my rudeness, my lord, but I scarcely knew where I was."

"Be seated, Dimitrios, and rest awhile, for you seem exhausted, then you may relate to us what has occurred."

The uproar in the streets appeared to have passed on, and it seemed to grow fainter as it withdrew to a greater distance. Dimitrios fell upon a seat, and, wiping his brow, began: "I was, this evening, walking along the Augustaeum, having been to St. Sophia, when I noticed a gathering of people opposite the palace of the Patriarch. They were gesticulating and vociferating wildly, and here and there I could distinguish the words: "Better the turban of the Turk in Constantinople than the Pope's tiara!"—I noticed several priests and monks, who were moving to and fro among the multitude, apparently haranguing them. Going up to an individual who seemed to be in a pensive mood, and who stood somewhat apart, I inquired the reason of the tumult. He informed me that the Emperor had issued an appeal to the people, begging for volunteers to defend the holy city, the centre of Eastern Christendom. About a quarter of an hour after my arrival, the Emperor had been seen to enter the "Royal Gate," on his return from St.

Sophia. A man at that moment began to address a few persons, standing at the beginning of the Augustaeum. The crowd gradually increased, until, worked up to a pitch of frenzy, by the harangue of the demagogue, it moved toward the palace of the Patriarch, denouncing him and the Emperor for their apostasy, and protesting that not a Grecian sword should be drawn in defense of the house of Paleologos. Suddenly there was a movement in the crowd, and the multitude rushed between St. Sophia and the Kathisma, through various other streets of the city, towards the "Golden Horn," with what object I know not. Caught in the vortex, I was carried along in the wild rush until, reaching your house, I managed to effect my escape."

"These unfortunate demagogues," said John Diogenes, they will be our ruin. The Emperor and the Patriarch have been unfaithful to our religion, it is true, but, here is a common cause, the fate of the Empire is at stake, all differences should be forgotten in the presence of the enemy. But, tell me, Dimitrios, did you hear the name of the man who worked thus upon the feelings of the people, and caused such a tumult?"

"I did not, my lord; in my pre-occupation I forgot to enquire, but you will pardon me if I say that I suspect."

"You suspect? And whom?"

"I suspect Nicolaus Lecapenos."

A frown passed over the brow of Diogenes, as he enquired: "You suspect Nicolaus, and why?"

"I cannot really say why, but an instinctive feeling tells me it was he."

"This is most unreasonable, Dimitrios. It is dangerous to be guided by imagination."

"I think I have reasons. I know how bitter Nicolaus

is against the Emperor and the Patriarch. You are acquainted with the power of his eloquence, moreover, a short time before the tumult, I met him on the Augustaeum, not far from the Patriarchal dwelling."

"These are far-fetched reasons, but, we shall see. Meanwhile, Dimitrios, I fain would exchange some words with you in private. Irene, withdraw, my child, and you, Basil, follow your sister."

Brother and sister, in obedience to their father's commands, after bidding Dimitrios good night, withdrew towards the inner part of the house, through the row of pillars on which the tapestry hung suspended. As Irene vanished behind the folds of the heavy curtain, she turned, and cast a look of deep sympathy on Dimitrios, who gazed after her in bewilderment, as though he would pierce the draperies with his look. Little did she dream, poor girl, of the sorrows that were in store for her, and that this was a last look she was casting upon him whom she called her betrothed. The night winds sighed, as though conscious of impending evil, and the gentle murmur of the waves could be heard, as, breaking upon the shore, they appeared to sing a melancholy chant. Dimitrios felt his heart sink within him, when he found himself alone with Irene's father, and a sharp presentiment of evil seemed to sting his soul. For a few seconds the two gazed at each other in silence, as if loth to begin. Finally, the elder spoke:

"You know how I have loved you. Your father, who now rests in the grave, was my bosom friend. On his deathbed, he begged me to watch over his infant son. Have I not been true to my trust?"

A tear stood in the eye of Dimitrios. With an astonished expression on his countenance, he exclaimed:

"My lord, my father, rather, what has occurred? Why ask that question?"

"Patience, Dimitrios, you shall hear. I have been for you a second father, and, in order to draw you still closer to myself, I have promised you my daughter in marriage, that daughter whom I love as the apple of my eye."

Dimitrios gazed, bewildered, at the speaker, who continued:

"Had I not a right to expect from you gratitude, at least fidelity, in return?"

Dimitrios was silent.

"Could I have dreamt that you would have deceived my daughter; in spite of all the affection I owed your father, never, no, never on earth, would you have crossed the threshold of this house. O! whom shall I trust, since my idol has fallen to the ground, and the angel of light has been changed into a spirit of evil!"

Dimitrios grew pale.

"This evening when you entered my house I received you kindly, I would not that Irene should notice what was passing in my mind. But, henceforth, you shall never meet her again, your serpent eye shall never again rest upon her pure form."

"My lord, what do you mean? I understand you not. Has any one—? Nicolaus, ah, yes, the demon!" and Dimitrios clenched his fist convulsively.

"I have not seen Nicolaus for two weeks. Vomit not your gall on his innocent head. I have other proofs, certain proofs, incontestable proofs, proofs which you cannot refute. I have the testimony of my dearest friend, who heard all from the lips of her whom you have chosen as your bride, while you make a dupe of my innocent daughter."

"But, my lord, explain, I am utterly ignorant of that to which you refer."

"You are ignorant! Yes, too long has the mask of hypocrisy covered your face. Begone from my presence, never to return!"

"But, may I not defend myself? Confront me with my accusers."

"Dimitrios, I will be just, your request shall be granted. On the twenty-fifth of next month, meet me at the Hippodrome, at the entrance to the imperial box, called the Kathisma, at two in the afternoon. Until then I decline to see your face."

"The twenty-fifth of next month! Alas! must I wait thus long? Who knows? It may be too late."

"It cannot be otherwise, it will be impossible for me to see the interested parties until then."

"And may I not see Irene, may I not bid her a last farewell?"

"Your eyes shall never fall on my daughter again. This is my final decision."

With this, the master of the house arose and pointed to the door. Dimitrios, with tottering limbs, withdrew. In a few moments he was in the street. The door of the house he loved so well, where he had spent so many happy moments, was closed upon him—closed forever. Silence reigned supremely, not a sound disturbed the stillness of the night save the gentle murmur of the wavelets, as they broke upon the shore, or the wind, as it swept past the forlorn youth, causing his locks to rise and fall in graceful ringlets on his shoulders. The stars looked silently down from the heavens, seeming to sympathize with the poor, suffering heart on earth, and reminding it that there is nothing steadfast, nothing true, but Heaven. For a long time Dimitrios stood, fixed in the same spot, with his eyes raised heavenward, as if unconscious of his own existence. His illusions had vanished, the earth seemed as naught, his spirit flew far away, and he exclaimed to himself: "Could I but share the solitude of Father Gregorios in his monastery of Agios Kyriani! I will seek him; to-morrow he leaves for Athens."

With these words he departed from the spot most loved on earth, a spot to which he had so freqently resorted, but which he was never to tread again. A moment, and Dimitrios had vanished into the gloom.

CHAPTER III.

The sun had risen high in the heavens, casting its rays upon the placid waters of the harbor which, in appearance, was converted into a sheet of polished silver, studded with diamonds. The light fell through the glazed windows of St. Sophia, scattering itself in various hues over all the objects in the vast edifice. A ray of violet, darting in a straight line from above the sanctuary, fell upon the face of a youth who knelt absorbed in prayer upon the marble floor. Dimitrios had spent a sleepless night and, before the dawn of day, had hastened to St. Sophia, for his heart in its utter loneliness, had turned instinctively to the companionship of Him who calls the weary to Himself and invites to come to Him all "who labor and are heavy burdened." For three hours he had been kneeling unconscious of his surroundings, when a manly hand was laid upon his shoulders and the monk Gregorios stood beside him. Dimitrios arose with a smile upon his countenance and the monk beckoned him to follow. They both left the temple at the western door and stood beside the covered passage built on arches and leading to the imperial palace.

"Dimitrios," said the monk, "I had hardly expected to see you again, but I am delighted to find you in the house of God. I suppose you were recommending your afflicted country to the Almighty. I am also pleased to notice that you do not share in the fanaticism of the populace, who have abandoned St. Sophia since the patriarch has been reconciled to Rome. After all, my son, for centuries we were in communion with the See of Rome and our greatest men, the Chrysostoms, the Gregorys, the Cyrils and the Basils, looked up with reverence to the Bishop of Old Rome. If we do not share in the communion of the Latin Church, nor take part in the services of those who have submitted to the Pope, there is no reason why our veneration for this ancient and venerable edifice should cease. Think you not so, Dimitrios?"

The latter, lost in revery, had scarcely understood the words of the monk. Suddenly startled in the midst of his thoughts, he could not conceal his embarrassment.

"You seem preoccupied," said the venerable man, "has anything occurred to disturb your tranquillity?"

"Father, I will accompany you to Athens."

"Accompany me to Athens, and why; what unexpected business calls you thither?"

"I have resolved to become a monk, to bury myself in your solitude of Agios Kyriani."

"To become a monk! Dimitrios, you are jesting, what sudden resolution is this?"

"I am in earnest, thoroughly in earnest. Disgusted with a world I can no longer love, I wish to leave it."

"But you spoke not thus yesterday. Have my words alarmed you, are you afraid of the Turks, will you fly from the enemy?"

"No, father, there is no fear in my heart, another motive power impels me."

"Confide in me, my son, you know I am your friend, what ails you?"

"Father, you are aware that I was bethrothed to Irene Diogenes."

"Aha! I suspected there was a love affair in this matter. Well, have you had a disagreement?"

"Not in the least, but her father——"

"Does her father object?"

"Most emphatically. Hear me."

Dimitrios here related the occurences of the previous evening, the monk listened attentively. When the former paused, he thus began:

"I understand your situation, I sound the depths of your feelings, but, believe me, all will be well in the end. This thought of becoming a monk is only the impulse of a moment, it comes not from God. You would wrong Irene were you to abandon her now, she is perfectly innocent of the whole affair, and, who knows? she may need your assistance in the perilous days that are impending. Take my advice, my son, and for the present, stay where you are. Remember your sister Helena, she has no one to depend upon but you, she was entrusted to you by your dying mother, would you abandon her in the hour of peril?"

The youth was silent, the image of his sister arose before him, and Irene, he could not forget Irene.

"If after six months," the monk continued, "you still persevere in your resolution to abandon the world and Helena has been provided for, come to me, I will see that the doors of Agios Kyriani be opened to receive you, and I, myself, will gladly welcome you."

"Thanks, father, thanks, I will abide by your decision and do nothing hastily."

"Well said, my son. Now I must leave you. Stay an instant, here comes the emperor with his suite."

At that moment there appeared a man whose countenance indicated that some momentous preoccupation weighed heavily upon him. He was clad in long robes richly embroidered in gold and on each of his shoes he wore a golden eagle. Accompanying him were ten noblemen of his court.

"How different from the ancient splendor of our emperor!" said the monk, "surely Byzantium is only a ghost of its former self." While he still spoke, the suite entered the church.

"Poor emperor!" exclaimed Dimitrios, "one can see that he suffers."

"My son, I must now bid you farewell," said the monk, "remember your promise, may God's blessing rest upon you!" With these words he embraced the youth and departed. Dimitrios re-entered the church.

It was the hour when the faithful were wont to assist at the Mass of the Presanctified which, during Lent, is celebrated daily instead of the Mass proper that, in the Greek Church, is offered during that holy season, only on Saturdays and Sundays. The edifice was singularly vacant, only here and there a solitary individual being discernible in some secluded nook or recess. The church itself, built in the form of a Greek cross, 241 feet long and 224 feet broad, seemed to stand there on the banks of the Bosphorus as a gigantic reminder of things that had been and a warning of things to come. It spoke of the distant past, when the great Constantine laid the foundations of the first St. Sophia, built probably in the style of the Basilicas, it told of its total destruction by fire on Easter night 404, the eve of the banishment of St. John Chrysostom, and how, when it had been rebuilt, it was once more burned to the ground during the riots at Constantinople, which took place in 532, in the reign of Justinian to whom the present glorious edifice owes its origin. A lofty dome, reaching to a height of 180 feet above the floor, and pierced by at least forty windows, surmounts the cross. The aisles and side apses are divided from the central spaces by magnificent colonnades of marble pillars brought from the ancient Pagan temples of Asia. The whole of the interior, both roof and dome, is covered with gilding or mosaics, but the day is not far distant when all that magnificence shall disappear beneath the whitewash brush of the fanatical Turks.

The emperor and his suite have taken their places in their magnificent stalls, the clergy has entered the sanctuary. The Patriarch officiates assisted by many of the clergy, among whom are present, the Protosyncellus, or Vicar-General, the Proto-Presbyter, or Archpriest, and the Chartophylax, or chancellor. The service takes place in the ancient Greeek tongue, and the liturgy used is that of St. John Chrysostom.

At the foot of the first pillar to the left of the altar, kneels one with whom we have been rendered acquainted, it is Dimitrios Phocas. The service is familiar to him, for it has undergone no change since the reconciliation with Rome, and the Latin Church has respected the venerable liturgies as well as the discipline of the Greeks. In his hand he holds a copy of the "*Eucologion*," which contains the service.

At the end of the office, when the emperor and his suite had left the church, Dimitrios arose to take his departure. As he reached the western door, he was brought face to face with the man who, the evening before, had been his informant concerning the riots on the great square, called the Augustaeum. Dimitrios recognizing him, bowed, when the stranger, smiling, exclaimed: "Ah! the young gentleman whom I had the honor of meeting last night!"

"The same," replied Dimitrios with a bow, and he added: "Can you tell me the name of him who aroused the populace to such a pitch?"

"I can," was the answer, "he bears the name of Nicolaus Lecapenos, but I think that he has been rendered harmless for a time, for an order has been issued for his arrest."

"I suspected as much," replied Dimitrios. "Are you a Greek, sir?"

"I am a Venetian; my name is Vincent Morosini."

"It is a great honor to me to form your acquaintance. I am Dimitrios Phocas."

"An illustrious name," said the Venetian, with a somewhat sarcastic smile.

Dimitrios noticed it and replied: "I think not that the blood of the usurper and tyrant Phocas flows in my veins, and, if it does, I repudiate the deeds of my inglorious ancestor."

"Well said, you are a true Greek. May I have the pleasure of your company this morning, if you are not otherwise engaged?"

Dimitrios bowed his thanks.

As they moved onward, Morosini spoke:

"I would be inclined to say that, like most Greeks, you will not wield the sword in defense of Constantinople, but the fact of your assisting at the office in St. Sophia, has caused me to doubt."

"Sir," replied Dimitrios, reddening, "I am a Greek,

and, as a Greek, I will remember my duty to my country; danger shall find me at my post."

"Bravo! give me your hand; henceforth we will be brothers. I go now to the Palace of the Emperor; of course, you accompany me."

"Will I be admitted to the Imperial presence?"

"Undoubtedly. You will be my companion. I have free access to the Emperor."

They had been moving in a northern direction, in front of the Church, when, turning to the right, they walked toward the east, between St. Sophia and the hospice of Sampson, until they reached the Chalcoprateion, or Brassmarket, whence they turned around St. Sophia, and walking in a southeastern direction, came to the Royal Gate, which gives admission to the enclosure, in the southern portion of which the Palace is situated.

"How sad!" exclaimed Dimitrios. "One may truly say, that Constantinople is in ruins. Everywhere the eye meets nothing but remnants of former magnificence; more than half of the city is unoccupied; our population, which was 700,000 in the year 500, has now dwindled down to a hundred thousand, most of whom dwell in great poverty; part of the porticoes of St. Sophia have fallen, and our people have not the means to make the necessary repairs, and now, behold! this great and noble Palace, with its grounds of 150 acres, its outer wall a mile long; this pride of our city, is so dilapidated, that the Imperial family only inhabits a mere corner of it. Alas! I fear the end is nigh."

"Too true," replied Morosini, "such is the fate of nations. Let us rest a while upon this broken column, an emblem of the decay of human institutions."

They both sat down in silence. The Venetian, gazing at the Palace, seemed lost in reflection; finally, he began:

"It is evident to every reflecting and unbiased mind, that the world's history has been developed according to a fixed and determined plan, and that the hand of a wisely-governing Providence appears throughout the entire course of the events that have occurred during the existence of man upon the earth. The same causes have universally been followed by the same effects, and there exists within the great variety of scenes enacted in the drama of history, a most perfect harmony. Nations, however much divergent from one another in manners, customs, laws and actions, all, more or less, resemble one another in the great outlines of their history. The invariable laws that seem to rule the course of human events are so fixed, that the world's past serves as a basis for conjecturing what the future will be. Nations were born, flourished and died, thus resembling the individuals of which they were composed; for there is a marked analogy between the life of nations and the life of individuals, and man, the microcosm, is a miniature image of the great world of which he forms a part.

"Some nations there are, with whose history we are, more or less, acquainted, that long since have ceased to be, whose birth remains wrapt in obscurity. Most of the ancient nations of the world, such as the Assyrians, Babylonians and Persians, belonged to this class. Others there are who still live on, either in a decrepit old age, as the remnant of the ancient Egyptians, or in the full strength and vigor that belonged to youthful days, like the inhabitants of Schythia. When we follow the history of nations, either those which are extinct, or those that still exist, we find that their prosperity, as well as their decay, is generally attributable to similar causes. This is true, not of separate nations alone, but also of an entire class of nations that form an existing state of society.

"Of man, before the Deluge, we know comparatively little; our investigations are limited to the nations that followed the great catastrophe. The peoples of the earth formed, after the Deluge, with the exception, perhaps, of the Assyrians, we find living in a barbarous, semi-barbarous or nomadic condition. Then, after many struggles, they attain to a period of great prosperity, in which the sun of their history seems to have reached its meridian. Finally, their glory declines; the very greatness of their civilization becomes the cause of their ruin. Weakened by internal dissensions, or excess of luxury, they easily fall a prey to strong, and often barbarous, nations; they are swept out of existence, or they mingle with their conquerors.

"Ancient Babylonia, developed, probably, from Turanian, Acadian and Semitic tribes, had reached a high degree of civilization in times most remote. Being conquered by Assyria, it regained its independence in the seventh century before Christ, and reached the height of its glory under Nebuchadnezzar II. The Babylonians were noted for their effeminacy, luxury and licentiousness, and this, no doubt, paved the way for the Persian dominion. Babylonia was conquered by Cyrus in 539 B. C.

"Assyria was, it appears, originally an offshoot of the Babylonian monarchy, It attained to a high degree of power, and, after the reign of Sennacherib, in the eighth century before Christ, gradually decayed, until it was destroyed about 606 B. C.

"Egypt, over the origin and the duration of which a veil of mystery hangs, was, after a succession of dynasties, and a series of conquests and defeats, subjugated by the Persians in 340 B. C., and it finally fell under the dominion of Alexander the Great, and, later, of the Ptolemies, in whose possession it remained until it was incorporated into the Roman Empire.

"The Medes and Persians, first separate peoples, were united by conquest, and they became one nation under Cyrus. Under Darius Hystaspes, the Persian Empire had reached its highest period of prosperity, but the reverses of fortune sustained in the struggle with Greece, under Xerxes, began its decadence. Under Darius III., it fell into the possession of Alexander the Great.

"This monarch, son of Philip of Macedon, conquered the world, and founded the short-lived Macedonian Empire. Most of the civilized countries of the world fell under his sceptre, and he pushed his conquests beyond the Indus. His return march from India was fatal. After his death, in 323 B. C., his vast empire, too vast to continue, was split up and divided among his Generals. Thus ended the power of Greece, that now made room for another and more lasting power, that of Rome.

Rome, from its humble beginning upon the banks of the Tiber, gradually grew to be the mistress of the world. The Roman eagle soared above almost all the nations of the earth, and overshadowed them with its wings. Under Augustus, it was at the very zenith of its glory; but, like the nations that had preceded it, the height of its prosperity was the beginning of its adversity.

The worm of luxury began to gnaw at the root of its civilization until the huge tree fell. When in the fifth century of our era, the barbarians from the north closed in around, and the steppes of Asia let loose their hordes upon it, the sturdy Romans of the days of the Republic no longer existed, and their degenerate descendants possessed neither the skill, the strength, nor the valor to resist the invaders. Centuries of licentiousness had rendered them completely powerless, and the Empire of the West disappeared in its turn from among the nations. Does it not seem to you that the turn of Byzantium has arrived? The empire of Constantine is in a state of irreperable decay, the barbarous Turks are before the walls, Byzantium shall fall, as Assyria, Babylonia, Persia, Macedonia and Rome fell, and I hold it for certain that the empire which began with a Constantine, shall end with a Constantine. Is there not a singular coincidence here? The founder of Rome was Romulus, and the founder of the Roman empire was Augustus. The last sovereign of Imperial Rome was another Romulus, with the diminutive name of Augustulus. The founder of Constantinople was Constantine, and it may be that his last successor will bear his name."

Dimitrios covered his face with his hands to hide the tears that were forcing themselves to his eyes. Morosini, noticing his emotion, continued: "Be not downcast, my friend; your country may fall, but Phœnix-like, the Grecian people may still arise from its ashes. Let us at least have the satisfaction of doing our duty. Come! We proceed."

Morosini and Dimitrios now directed their steps towards the palace. The guards at the entrance, recognizing the Italian, allowed him to pass. Walking towards a door with which he seemed familiar, Morosini whispered to an attendant who admitted him into a spacious apartment. The floor consisted of mosaics, while the marble walls and gilded ceiling gave evidence of the splendor which once belonged to the palace of the Byzantine emperors. In this room they waited for a short time, when a door opened, and a richly-clad servant entered and, bowing, invited them to follow him. Ascending a flight of stairs and passing through a wide corridor, they reached an arched door which admitted them nto a magnificent hall. Its decorations greatly resembled those of the former apartment, but at one end of the room there stood a gilded throne upon an elevated platform, over which a rich canopy of red and gold hung suspended. It was the first time that Dimitrios had entered within the precincts of the imperial palace, and he stood breathlessly awaiting the arrival of the emperor. Finally the door opened, and the body guard of the sovereign entered, followed by the monarch himself. The guards drew up in two lines, facing each other, while the emperor walked between them towards the visitors, who both knelt before him. Bidding them arise, the emperor took each by the hand as he spoke: "In the common misfortunes that befall our country, we suspend the rules of etiquette. Morosini, who is this young man?"

"One of Your Majesty's most faithful subjects," replied the Italian, "one who is determined to stand or fall with Constantinople."

The emperor's eyes twinkled. Grasping the young man by the hand, he asked: "Have you ever borne arms, my son?"

"Never, Your Majesty," he replied.

"You will soon be proficient, I see it in your manly bearing. I appoint you a member of my guard, henceforth you will be attached to my own person. But of this later. Morosini have you a communication to make?"

"I have, Sire, but for your ear alone is it intended." Hereupon the emperor withdrew the Italian to a distance and listened as he spoke.

"Sire, Nicolaus Lecapenos, whose arrest you have ordered, has gone over to the Turkish camp. He left the city secretly by water, and, before taking his departure, he communicated his design to a friend, through whose indiscretion the matter has leaked out."

"Traitor!" exclaimed the emperor, "on whom shall we rely? But, tell me, have I been too hasty in appointing this young man? May we depend upon him?"

"Your Majesty, I can vouch for him, I have been acquainted with him for some time, though he knew it not, though he had never seen me until last night. I have watched him carefully; unseen by him, I have overheard his conversations. I am convinced of his patriotism. Nicolaus Lecapenos, while pretending to be his friend, is his mortal enemy."

"Enough," said the emperor, "he has my confidence. I thank you for the information conveyed to me. Should Lecapenos again enter the city, his life shall pay for his desertion. I rely on you to report to me anything of importance that may occur."

Morosini bowed and the emperor turned toward Dimitrios, saying in a loud voice: "Introduce the young man to the chieftain of the guards, to whom I myself will transmit special orders concerning him. But, what is his name?"

"Dimitrios Phocas," replied Morosini.

"Well, Dimitrios," said the emperor, "show thyself a true son of Byzantium."

The emperor smiled upon the two men, and turning, withdrew in the midst of his soldiers.

In a few moments, Morosini and Dimitrios were in the streets where they parted, promising to meet in the afternoon, to proceed together to the quarters of the imperial guards.

CHAPTER IV.

The day was nearly spent, the rays of the sun descended obliquely towards the earth, fleecy clouds soared high in the heavens, while huge masses of vapor gathered above the horizon toward the East where the Black Sea washed the shores of what was once the Byzantine Empire, which had now, almost entirely, succumbed to the Turkish power. Far out towards the West, the eye discerned the towers of Adrianople, over which the sun still lingered as though loth to part with another day, which he was soon to lose forever. At that moment another sun was setting, the sun of Byzantium's life. Internal dissensions, treachery and vice had done their work and the empire was approaching its end. A solitary horseman was seen pursuing his way in the direction of the city. He rode a fiery Arab steed, causing the earth to tremble beneath its hoofs, while here and there a flock of birds flew upward from a neighboring bush, frightened from their retreat by the unwonted sound. The country seemed deserted, no other human-being was in sight and the fertile acres appeared to have been for a long time neglected. Above the walls of the city, floated the triumphant standard of Mahomet. The solitary rider, spurring his horse, muttered to himself: "I must reach it before the gates are closed." His horse, foaming at the mouth, dashed onward scarcely touching the earth and seeming rather to fly than to run. The city grew more distinct, its fortifications and walls standing out in strong relief against the sky. The sun sank lower, the day was fast declining, the gates would soon be closed. Onward rushed the rider, heedless of all save the goal of his journey. Persons were seen to move within the city's eastern gate which was now a stone's throw away. A Turk, with drawn scimitar, advanced. Approaching within speaking distance, he exclaimed in the Turkish language:

"Halt."

Obedient to the command, the rider drew the reins of his horse.

"Who art thou?" asked the Turk.

"A friend. I come from Constantinople, I am the bearer of important news."

These words were spoken in the same language.

"A Greek!" exclaimed the follower of the prophet in a low voice, "a Greek who speaks the Turkish tongue, probably sent to sue for peace. But no! an ambassador would hardly come alone."

"Advance, stranger." The rider, gently touching his horse, proceeded trotting towards the Turk over whose face a sign of recognition suddenly passed, while his rude countenance displayed a ferocious grin, intended for a smile.

"Ah! Nicolaus Lecapenos, hast thou come at last? The Sultan has threatened to strike off thy head, if thou should'st have delayed twenty-four hours longer."

"I am delighted at having escaped the danger, but the Grand Seignor may also thank his stars, for he would have lost one of his best and most useful subjects."

"We want no impertinence, Christian dog, take heed

to thy words," and with this the Mahomedan brandished his sword.

"Why call me a Christian; have I not embraced the religion of the Prophet?"

"Yes, hypocrite, to serve thy own base purposes, but"—and here he spoke in lower tones—"thou dost believe as much in the Prophet as I do, who was born a Christian in the far-off North, but whom circumstances have turned into a Turk."

"Take thou heed to thy own words, Selim, or I will have thy headless trunk thrown to the ravens ere to-morrow's sun gilds the minarets of yonder mosque."

"I mock thy words, Nicolaus, it is in my power to have thy head exposed to the scorn of all the faithful from the summit of this very gate. Dost thou remember Leila, the maiden, half Greek and half Italian, who lives in Constantinople? I know what thou did'st say to her. Did'st thou not assert that were it to thy advantage, and were Prince Orkhan to revolt to-morrow against the Sultan, thou would'st not hesitate to join his standard, that thou carest neither for Sultan, Emperor nor Pope, but only for thy own dear self? Well, if thou carest for thy own dear self, take heed how thou speakest to me."

Nicolaus, evidently embarrassed, exclaimed:

"Come Selim, let us be friends."

"As long as it suits my purpose, young man."

With these words he beckoned Nicolaus to follow. Entering the city, the Greek alighted from his horse, which he fastened to a post. Following Selim into a doorway beside the gate, he seated himself on a stone bench.

"Well, Selim,' he began, "is everything favorable?"

"You should know that better than I."

"So be it then. When do you think that I can see the Sultan?"

"This very night. I will inform him immediately of thy arrival."

Hereupon Selim withdrew, leaving Nicolaus to his reflections. A long time passed, which seemed an eternity to the Greek, the minutes appearing to have grown into hours. Finally the door opened and Selim appeared. Beckoning to Nicolaus, he said:

"Follow me, the Sultan desires thy presence."

Arising, the latter proceeded to untie his horse, but he was prevented by Selim, who said:

"I will take care of the animal, go thou hence with these two soldiers who will direct thee."

The men indicated, preceded Nicolaus in silence until they reached the front of a large palace. Entering the arched doorway they whispered to a servant and Nicolaus was conducted by them to an anteroom, where he was left to himself. The apartment was almost devoid of furniture, there being in it neither chairs nor tables, though magnificent rugs were everywhere spread upon the floor. After waiting a few moments, he was summoned to appear before the Sultan. Suddenly a large folding door opened as if by magic, and he found himself at the entrance of an immense hall, which was literally flooded with the light of innumerable torches. On both sides of the room Turkish guards stood in line with drawn scimitars which flashed in the glare of the artificial light. At various distances from one another were seated on carpets dignitaries of the court with their legs crossed. At the opposite extremity of the hall, and seated in the same attitude, was a man in the full vigor of youth. His countenance bore the marks of the most arrogant pride, his nose was aquiline, his lips sensual, and his eyes cruel. He was clad in Turkish style, with wide trousers drawn together at the feet, while over his shoulders hung a rich mantle worked in gold. In the front of his turban sparkled a precious stone of enormous size, inlaid in the same metal.

As his eyes fell upon the Greek, they twinkled with an expression of cunning, mingled with pleasure. The newcomer being led into the presence of the Turkish Majesty, fell prostrate upon the ground. At the bidding of the Sultan, he arose.

"Thou hast at last arrived," spoke the Monarch, "but leave thy excuses for another time, make haste and relate what thou hast learned."

"In Constantinople," replied Nicolaus, "the greatest discontent prevails with the Emperor and the patriarch, I myself have helped to foster it. The population is in a state of apathy; nearly all have turned a deaf ear to the appeal of the Sovereign, and only two thousand Greek volunteers have consented to join the defenders of the city, the number of whom is known to you. The time is now ripe, strike one blow and Constantinople shall fall."

"That blow shall soon be struck," replied the Sultan. "The Emperor has appealed to my clemency in behalf of his remnant of an Empire, but appeals are now useless. The Cross must yield to the Koran, Mahomet shall rule in Constantinople. First, however, thou hast a mission to fulfill. To-morrow thou must return to that city."

The countenance of Nicolaus fell. Trembling, he exclaimed: "Return to that city. I will never leave it alive, for the Emperor has ordered my arrest."

"Thou shalt go in disguise."

"So be it," answered Nicolaus, "and what shall my mission be?"

"Thy mission shall be to foster the spirit of discontent among the people. Thou shalt remain in Constantinople until the Turkish army has entered. If thou succeedest, the Greek beauty on whom thou hast set thy heart, shall be thine; if not, thy head shall fall. Thou mayst now retire."

Nicolaus again prostrated himself before the Sultan, and, conducted by two guards, left the palace.

It was night when he reached the house of Selim, who awaited him.

"Well, Greek," said the Mahometan, "how didst thou fare?"

"Badly enough," was the reply, "I must return to Constantinople. They will kill me like a dog, and throw my carcase to the birds of prey."

"The world will be well rid of thee."

Nicolaus frowned, but repressed his anger.

"Tell me, Selim, he asked, "how didst thou know Leila?"

"There is very little in Constantinople that I know not, thou art not the only spy in the world. It matters not how I know Leila, sufficeth for thee that I know her. Thou hast made her thy tool, but that tool may some day cut thee. Thou hast used her lying tongue to injure young Dimitrios Phocas, thou didst even endeavor to employ her to ingratriate thyself with the Byzantine Court, and thou wouldst have been willing to betray the cause of the Turk, had the Greeks consented to remunerate thee according to thy desires. But the Emperor knows all now, and thou wilt do well if thou dost escape from Byzantium with thy life."

"Heavens! Selim, thy knowledge astounds me. It is useless to enquire from what source it has been derived, I see that I am between two fires, but thou wilt be my friend, wilt thou not?"

"I have told thee once that I would, as long as it suits my purpose, but beware lest thou offend me."

"Thou shalt not have to complain of me, Selim. But I must go, to-morrow's sun shall find me on my way to Constantinople. Farewell!"

Nicolaus now departed to the house of a friend, where he was to spend the night.

The next morning, long before daybreak, he had left the city, an order from the Sultan having procured the opening of the gates. As he journeyed along, he thus mused within himself:

"Infamous Turk! he has discovered my secret. Gladly would I tie a stone around his neck and bury it with him under the waters of the Bosphorus. But I will have my revenge. Nicolaus, would it not be better for thee to throw thyself upon the mercy of the Emperor, and reveal to him the plans of the Sultan? But no! thy life would be in still greater danger, for Constantinople will certainly fall, and thou wouldst lose thy head. Even didst thou live, the coveted reward would not be thine, thou wouldst not possess Irene. Take courage, Nicolaus, the danger is great, but the reward is greater."

Thus conversing with himself, Nicolaus Lecapenos proceeded on his way to Constantinople, until, deviating from the straight road, after a long journey, he reached the Turkish fort, on the Bosphorus, where a letter from the Sultan assured him a most cordial welcome. Here we leave him, to follow the events transpiring in Constantinople.

CHAPTER V.

"Father, father! Come quickly!" exclaimed a voice from the courtyard of the house of John Diogenes.

"What ails thee, my son?" sounded the reply from the inner portion of the building, and, at the same time, Diogenes stepped out into the court where, beside a fountain, knelt Basil, with his hand on the forehead of his sister, Irene, who evidently had swooned.

"Poor child!" exclaimed the father, "she has grown exceedingly weak."

Indeed, whosoever had seen Irene when, a few days before, seated at her father's feet, she drank in his words, as he spoke of the history of Constantinople, would hardly have recognized her now. Her eyes were sunken; the roses had faded from her cheeks; the springtide of joy had vanished from her life, and it was evident that the cold, dreary, winter of some intense sorrow had settled upon her. Kneeling beside his child, and bathing her forehead with the cool water of the fountain, Diogenes endeavored to recall her to consciousness. Finally, his efforts seemed successful, and she opened her eyes, which had lost all their fire, and become dull and languid. Allowing them to wander hither and thither, with a puzzled expression on her face, she moaned in a low voice: "Dimitrios," and again closed her eyes.

"My child, do not you know me?" said her father.

The young girl opened her eyes and allowed them to rest with a languid expression upon his face.

"You are tired, my dear," he said, "and need rest. Basil, send for a litter."

In a few moments the boy returned, with two servants, who carried a litter, upon which they gently placed the girl, then bore her into the house, followed by Diogenes and his son. The young lady was taken to a room and laid upon a magnificent couch, while a female attendant was summoned to wait upon her. Gradually, her strength seemed to return, but the color came not to her wan cheeks; the roses seemed to have faded forever. Her father sat by her side, looking anxiously at her. Basil entered the room and whispered:

"Father, there is an aged pilgrim in the atrium, who says that he desires to see you."

"I will come instantly, my son, meanwhile stay with your sister, but remain very quiet."

The father now proceeded to the atrium, where his eyes fell upon a man of venerable mien, whose white locks descended to his shoulders, while a full beard, of immaculate whiteness, reached his chest. He was clad in the garb of a pilgrim, a broad hat hung upon his back, and he leaned upon a staff, as though worn out by his travels. As his eye fell upon the master of the house, he bowed profoundly.

"Holy man," spoke the former, "I bid thee welcome to my hospitable dwelling. No doubt, thou hast come from a distance, and needest rest and refreshment; thou shalt find both under my roof."

"A thousand thanks; may the Virgin Mother of Christ protect thee!" replied the aged man, in a feeble voice, "I have been refreshed, and the pangs of hunger have been stilled, but I will gladly accept thy hospitality, and may it be in my power to reward thee!"

"Hast thou been to the Holy Places, venerable pilgrim?"

"I have just returned from Jerusalem, and I am now proceeding to my own country, Burgundy."

"You are a Frank? But you speak our language perfectly."

"I am a Frank, but I hope that our difference of creed will not cause me to be less acceptable in your sight. I love the Greeks. I have traveled much in the Levant, and there I learned to speak your beautiful language."

"May I inquire into the nature of your profession, holy father?"

"I am a physician; I learned the art in the Monastic Schools of Italy."

"A physician; thank God! You are thrice welcome. You must know, I have a daughter; a beautiful girl; an angel. For some time she has sickened and wasted away. The least fatigue or emotion, causes her to faint. Only this morning I found her in a swoon. The men versed in the science of medicine, whom I have consulted, have been unable to console me. The disease seems to baffle their skill. Perhaps, Providence has sent you to this house to relieve the heart of a disconsolate man."

"It may be in my power to afford some relief, and I will be infinitely happy thus to repay your hospitality. May I see the lady?"

"Undoubtedly. Follow me."

Diogenes led the way, accompanied by the pilgrim. Entering the room of his daughter, he spoke:

"I have brought you a friend; a physician; a holy man, who has just returned from a visit to Palestine. He will cure you."

The stranger approached. Irene smiled faintly, but as her eye fell upon the face of the pilgrim, she experienced an indescribable feeling of antipathy. The holy man took her hand and felt her pulse; its beating was weak, but rapid. He gazed at her countenance, looked into her eyes, and smiled.

"She will recover," said he to her father, "if you follow the directions I will give. Meanwhile, she must be kept quiet, and no one must be allowed to see her."

Turning to Irene, he said:

"Young lady, I will see thee again."

He bowed and left the room, followed by her father. When they were alone, the pilgrim spoke:

"You know that the Turks are approaching nearer to this city. A long siege will ensue, and I assure you that, besides the danger to which your daughter will be exposed, if the city falls, the excitement of a long siege will be fatal to her in her present weak condition. Have you a villa removed some distance from Constantinople?"

"I have a splendid villa in Attica."

"You have? The climate of Attica is delightful—a perpetual spring reigns there; rain is rare, and a cloudy day is seldom seen. There could be no better place for your daughter than Attica. Remove her at once, if you value her life."

"But the whole country is in the hands of the Turks; such a journey could not be undertaken without danger."

"Not the least danger exists. I am a friend of the

Pasha who commands the Turkish fort on the Bosphorus. I have rendered him great services, and he is in my debt. I will obtain a guard to accompany you and your daughter."

Diogenes regarded the pilgrim with a look of diffidence.

"You need not be alarmed," spoke the latter. "I see no other way of saving your daughter's life. It will be certain death for her to remain in Constantinople. I will follow you after a few days."

"I would like to reflect," said Irene's father.

"Delay is dangerous. After the siege begins, it will be impossible to depart. You must go now, or sacrifice your daughter."

"Well, so be it. I will give orders immediately to prepare for the journey, but how shall we travel?"

"A vessel sails to-morrow morning for Athens; embark upon it. I will give directions to the Captain; he will land not far from the Turkish fort; the guard will come on board; the vessel carrying you will hoist a signal flag, understood by the Turks, and you will pass without risk through the fleet of the enemy. After landing at Piraeus, your daughter can finish the rest of the journey in a litter."

"But, will the Captain of the vessel consent to undertake this expedition?"

"I will arrange all with him," answered the pilgrim; "he must, at all events, leave to-morrow. I know him well, for it was on his vessel that I arrived from Smyrna, and it is owing to me that he was enabled to pass the Turks."

"But will there not be a danger from the side of our own ships?"

"No! for you will carry the Grecian flag until you have left the harbor. Moreover, the vessel is destined for Venice, and is the bearer of important despatches from the Greek Government. Of this the Turks know nothing. Thus, you see, that there is naught to fear, neither on the side of the Greeks, nor on that of the Turks."

"As you say, then, to-morrow morning we will be in readiness. Can you not accompany us?"

"Not now, for important business detains me in Constantinople, but I will follow you in a few days."

"But, if the siege begins before that time, how will you leave the city?"

"My character of a pilgrim will insure respect on the part of the Greeks, while my credit with the Turks, will enable me to cross the lines."

"Holy Father, I dare say you are fatigued; will you not retire to rest?"

"I must leave you awhile," the pilgrim replied, "for my time is short, but I will return before midnight. I would, however, see your daughter ere I depart. Will you accompany me to her room?"

"With pleasure," said Diogenes, as he led the way.

Entering the room of Irene, they found her asleep. Suddenly startled in the midst of her slumbers, she exclaimed:

"Dimitrios, where art thou?"

The hermit shuddered. He felt the pulse of the girl, spoke reassuringly to her father, and both left the room.

"Does she often speak while in a semi-conscious condition?" asked the pilgrim.

"Yes, and her thoughts always seem to revert to the same subject, her betrothed, namely, Dimitrios Phocas."

"Oh! Is the young lady to be married? And to whom did you say?"

"She was engaged to one Dimitrios Phocas, but I have caused the engagement to be broken."

The eyes of the hermit sparkled with unwonted fire, which was not unnoticed by Diogenes, who asked:

"Do you know Dimitrios Phocas?"

"I know not the young man in person, but I was well acquainted with his father, whom I met in Asia. On my return to this city, I inquired concerning the family, but what I have heard is not reassuring. And you say that Dimitrios was betrothed to your beautiful daughter? Did you know the young man?"

"I believed him the very soul of honor, but, alas! I have been cruelly undeceived. Have you heard aught in his favor?"

"Would that it were in my power to pour the balm of consolation upon your afflicted soul! I fear, however, that I can say nothing that would raise Dimitrios in your esteem."

"Do you know anything in regard to him?"

"Your kindness towards me, a perfect stranger, and the interest I take in the welfare of your daughter, constrain me to speak, though I would much prefer to observe a charitable silence. But I must here sacrifice my inclination to the duty I owe you. I have been informed, from reliable sources, that Dimitrios has sunk very low. He frequents the most degraded resorts; he is the friend of gamblers and low women, and, what is worse, he has agreed to marry the most infamous courtesan in the city, the degraded Leila. Did you know this?"

"I had heard as much. Oh, my daughter! my poor daughter! I fear this will kill her."

"Fear not, my good friend; under the bright skies of Attica, your child will regain her strength; she will learn to forget, and when she knows the true state of the matter, she will thank you for having delivered her from the clutches of the monster. Meanwhile, begin your preparations, for time is short. Farewell until morning."

Long before the sun arose over Constantinople, a small vessel had weighed anchor and steered for the passage between the inner harbor and the Bosphorus. It contained a crew of twenty-five men, who had their quarters in the forecastle, besides five officers and a Captain, who had surrendered their berths in the after cabin to Diogenes, his daughter, Irene, and his son, Basil. The craft carried two small cannon at the bow, while the balls were kept in a box, fastened to the bulwarks. These balls were not of iron, but of stone. From her mizzen-top floated the Standard of Byzantium.

At the moment when the vessel reached the entrance to the outer harbor, a youth might have been seen standing on the shore at the landing place, clad in the uniform of the Emperor's Guards. His hands were folded before him, with the palms turned downward, while his eyes anxiously followed the vessel through the gloom of the morning. Beside him stood the pilgrim, whom we yesterday met in the house of Diogenes. He seemed engaged in endeavoring to console the young man. Had you approached near enough, you might have overheard the following conversation:

"Had I known where to find thee, my son, I might

have informed thee, and a reconciliation might have been effected."

Dimitrios moved not his eyes from the vessel, which receded further from him. He seemed riveted to the spot, and he felt that the dearest object to him in life, was being carried further away. He had lost all ambition, and, for the moment, he cared not whether Constantinople stood or fell. One only star shone brightly above the darkness of his soul, the star of his faith; he felt that even if he lost the creature, nothing could ever deprive him of the Creator, and, in proportion to the loneliness of his heart, his soul soared upward to a higher and a better life

The pilgrim regarded him in silence, and repeated:

"Had I but known where to find thee!"

"Do you say that Irene believes me guilty?"

"I do; it is unfortunately thus. I endeavored to convince her of thy innocence, assuring her that I had heard the most favorable reports concerning thee, but it was all in vain. She solemnly asserted that she would never lay eyes on thee again."

A tempest raged within the bosom of the young man. Love, despair, rage, revenge, mingled their loud cries within his agonized heart, casting their echoes alternately upon his beautiful face. Suddenly, as though impelled by some secret power, he darted from the side of the pilgrim. He was gone.

The silent pillars of St. Sophia, that in ages past had been witness of so much virtue, so much suffering, and so much treachery, now alone heard the pent-up sighs that burst forth from the heart of Dimitrios Phocas. The morning breeze, wafted through the windows of the Temple, caught up his prayers and seemed to bear them to the Throne above.

The sun cast its fair rays over the city; the birds flew upward from the branches of the trees; the little boats glided over the waters of the Golden Horn; merry children played on the Augustaeum; all nature seemed to rejoice; one heart was sad, for a gulf seemed to yawn between Dimitrios and Irene.

CHAPTER VI.

In a small house in one of the most remote quarters of Constantinople, sat a young woman. The appearance of the dwelling, though not wretched, was indicative of poverty, and the furniture seemed to have witnessed better days. Her costume was neglected, while her hair hung loose over her shoulders; but against the wall, a dress of costly material and most gaudy ornamentation was suspended. Her face was pale, while a smile on her lips seemed to denote an artful nature. Still there was something about this woman's countenance which indicated that it had once known refinement, innocence and joy. She was unoccupied, staring into vacancy, with her head resting on her hand, while her elbow leaned on a table, when the door suddenly opened, and our pilgrim entered. The girl sprang up startled. The visitor saw her look of dismay, and exclaimed:

"Leila, dost thou not know me?"

In a moment his hair and long beard lay on the floor and Nicolaus Lecapenos stood before her. She gave a shriek of surprise and fell back upon her chair. Nicolaus, seating himself spoke:

"I have been ordered to return to Constantinople and remain here until the city falls. My life is in constant danger, but it cannot be otherwise. However, I must ask you a question. Do you know a Turk called Selim?"

"I know a Turk! How could I know a Turk?"

"But he knows you."

"A Turk knows me! Nicolaus, you are dreaming."

"Most assuredly I am not. Come, tell me the truth, do you not know Selim?"

"By all that is sacred, I never heard the man's name."

"But he knows all that I have told you, concerning Dimitrios, and in regard to the Emperor and the Sultan. Have you no confidants, did you never mention my conversation to others?"

Leila appeared embarrassed. After a moment's reflection, she replied:

"Where did you tell me those things? Was it not in the Hippodrome? Did I not beg you to be prudent and not raise your voice? May you not have been overheard?"

A sudden light seemed to flash before the eyes of Nicolaus. "Could it be possible?" he exclaimed.

"How is Dimitrios Phocas?" said Leila, endeavoring to turn the conversation.

"How Dimitrios is? He is safe, and Irene is safe; she is far away by this time."

"Far away, what do you mean?"

"She has left the city, and she is now on her way to Attica, as her father thinks. Ah! I have caught the bird, thanks to you, Leila."

"Yes, thanks to me. Not content with having wrecked my life, you make me a tool for all your wicked plans. Nicolaus, you know that I was once innocent, I dreamt not of malice. but you have dragged me down into the lowest depths of degradation, ruining both body and soul. Gloat not, I pray you, over the tortures of your victim, let me go now, give me my liberty."

"Give you your liberty? As if I were the only one who held you captive."

"O, Nicolaus, this is cruel. I avow that I am wretched, wicked, if you like, but remember that you are the first cause of it all."

"Hush, insolent harlot, or—" and he clutched at a dagger.

Leila buried her face in her hands and wept.

"Have you no pity, Nicolaus?" she moaned.

"None for such as you are," he replied.

She looked at him, and a mysterious fire darted from her eyes. He recoiled in terror.

"Tigress," he exclaimed, flashing his dagger before her eyes, "do you threaten me?"

"Strike, monster, strike; death would be a thousand times preferable to such a life. I am an outcast; the world which at heart is no better than myself, spurns me; those whose toy I am, look on me with contempt. What have I to live for?"

"No, I will not strike, you are too useful to me, and when I no longer need you, there are more than enough Turks to whom I can sell you."

With a roar that frightened even Nicolaus, the infuriated woman, no longer recognizable, dashed at her persecutor, she plunged her nails into his face, she would have torn him to pieces, but Nicolaus, holding her aloof with the left hand, raised the right, the dagger flashed, and, in another moment, it was buried in the bosom of the unfortunate woman. She fell, and, in falling, she exclaimed:

"Righteous God, Thy justice has overtaken me, be Thou merciful to my soul!"

The words died on her lips, the tongue that had uttered them was silent. Thus fell a young girl, who, born in the bosom of refinement, and educated in innocence, had, in a weak moment, lent an ear to the words of the basilisk. She had gone from bad to worse, this was the end.

Nicolaus, full of consternation at his work, for the whole had been effected almost before he had time to reflect, hurried to the street, hoping to evade observation, but, in his haste, he forgot that he was without his wig and beard. No sooner had he reached the street than he discovered his error; he quickly turned on his heels, but, to his consternation, he fell into the arms of a man, who exclaimed:

"Ah! holy pilgrim, art thou here? But what sudden change has come over thee? Thou hast lost thy beard, and hast thou dyed thy hair?"

Nicolaus was speechless with terror.

"Hast thou not a word for an old acquaintance?" asked Morosini, for it was he.

"Let me go," moaned Nicolaus.

"Let thee go? No, dear boy, one does not let game escape which throws itself so easily into the net. But what hast thou been doing in this house?"

Morosini dragged his unwilling captive toward the door. As he crossed the threshold, he stepped back, horror stricken. Leila's corpse lay on the floor, in a pool of blood.

"Monster," he exclaimed, "vile monster, is this the end of thy victim?"

"I could not help it," stammered Nicolaus, "she would have killed me," and, as he said these words, with a sudden movement he reached for the dagger that lay on the floor. Morosini divined his intention, and, with a giant grasp, held him back, at the same time, drawing his sword.

"Dare to move hand or foot, without my permission, wretch, and this blade shall divide thy accursed heart in twain."

The coward trembled.

Vincent Morosini knelt beside the victim, he sought for signs of life, he endeavored to detect the slightest movement of the heart, but all in vain. He shook his head sadly. Life was extinct. "Traitor, murderer, fiend!" he exclaimed, as he cast a look of contempt and indignation upon Nicolaus. Then, his face assuming a softer expression, he said:

"Poor girl! I knew her father and mother in Pera. They died broken-hearted. And this is the wreck, this is all that is left of the once beautiful and innocent Angela Ladrazzoni!"

CHAPTER VII.

While the dreadful scene, described in our last chapter, was being enacted in the city of Constantinople, a small bark was struggling with the waves on the Sea of Marmora. It had experienced no difficulty in passing the Grecian fleet, and, by means of a signal flag, agreed upon between Nicolaus and the Turkish Pasha while the former was in the fort, it had, also, passed safely through the Turkish ships. After a short sail towards the north, in the direction of the Euxine or Black Sea, it had touched at the European shore of the Bosphorus, where a guard of twelve men had come on board. Turning towards the south, and setting all sail, it had then headed directly for the Propontis and the Hellespont, or Dardanelles.

The Turks were most respectful in their conduct towards Irene and her father, but the former could not repress a feeling of horror that came over her as she looked upon the ferocious faces of the followers of Mahomet, and she thought of the deeds of blood that had accompanied all their marches.

His daughter was the object of the constant solicitude of John Diogenes; he never left her side, and did all that a paternal heart might suggest to relieve her sufferings. In fine weather he would conduct her to the poop, and point out to her the various portions of the landscape he thought might be of interest to her. At the distance of a few leagues from the Bosphorus, they encountered a storm, which caused their vessel to pitch and roll, while the waves washed over her deck. Both Basil and his father succumbed to sea-sickness, but Irene appeared not in the least affected. A deeper affliction weighed upon her. She was being carried far from home, in obedience to her father's wishes, but against her own inclination. However, she murmured not, but bore her sorrow in silence.

For nearly twenty-four hours they labored with the storm, but, as they reached the Dardanelles, the fury of the wind abated, and the weather grew calmer. Passing through the narrow straits, they could see the land on both sides. On the left lay the coast of Asia Minor, while on the right they beheld the shores of Greece. It was in the early morning when they ran out into the Archipelago. The mariner's needle had, most probably, for several centuries, been applied to navigation, and, though the vessel, on board which sailed the Diogenes family, possessed this instrument, yet, to avoid any possible error, the Captain determined to sail along the southern shores of what is now known as Turkey. On the next morning they had reached the Gulf of Thessalonica, and the Captain was about to turn his helm to starboard, in order to sail along the Grecian coast, towards Athens, when the Chieftain of the Turkish Guard advanced toward him, and, in a respectful tone, said:

"Captain, will you oblige me by turning into the Gulf?"

"I cannot," replied the Captain; "my destination is Athens."

"You may go to Athens, but you must first proceed to Thessalonica; after that we will offer no further hindrance to your plans."

"By whose orders do you thus command me?"

"By orders of the Pasha."

"And, suppose I decline to obey?"

"We will take charge of the ship ourselves."

"But, if we prevent you?"

"We shall use force."

"But we are more numerous than you; we are two to one."

"We shall see. I warn you, Captain, not to interfere with my orders, for, if you do, though you conquer us, your ship can never enter these waters again."

The Captain reflected. After a moment's silence, he spoke:

"And what calls you to Thessalonica?"

"All I can say is, that I have orders to proceed to Thessalonica."

The Captain of the vessel, without replying, ordered the helm reversed, and the ship swung around towards the Gulf.

John Diogenes, advancing towards the Captain, enquired:

"Captain, whither are we going?"

"To Thessalonica."

"I thought you were bound for Athens?"

"I am bound for Athens, but we must first put in at Thessalonica."

Diogenes made no reply, but a sense of uneasiness came over him.

A few hours' sailing up the Gulf, brought them in sight of the city. Basil now came on deck and advanced toward his father, who was standing beside Irene, the latter apparently indifferent to all that was passing.

"Father," said the boy, pointing to the city, the white houses of which could be distinctly seen, "is that Athens?"

"No, my son, not yet. That is Thessalonica."

"What are we going to do there?"

"I cannot say; the Captain tells us that he must put in at this city, before proceeding to Athens."

They were fast approaching the city. A Turkish vessel, sighting them, came alongside. The Turkish Chieftain exchanged a few words in his language with the commander of the newcomer, who, hereupon, fell astern, following the Greek.

The former now proceeded to the Captain of the vessel and thus addressed him:

"Captain, you have despatches for Venice?"

"I have not," was the answer; "you have been misinformed."

"My information is correct. If you surrender the despatches, you may proceed; if not, we hold you prisoners."

"I have no despatches," said the Greek.

"Then I cannot allow you to proceed until your persons, and every nook and corner of your vessel have been searched."

With these words, he withdrew to a distance. The Greek vessel now cast anchor. Two Turkish boats came alongside. The Captain of the Guard, bowing before Diogenes, said:

"I have orders to land you at Thessalonica."

"From whom?" asked the Greek, in surprise.

"From the Pasha."

A light began to dawn upon Diogenes. For some reason or other, he had been betrayed. Resistance, he felt, was utterly useless. His sole uneasiness arose from the contemplation of his daughter's danger. At all events, he would quiet her fears, and cause her to believe that he had come to Thessalonica from choice. If it came to the worst, he was determined to defend her life and honor to the bitter end.

When everything was in readiness, the three Greeks left the vessel and entered one of the Turkish boats, which conveyed them to land, while the other boat followed with the guards.

In the few years since its capture, Thessalonica had been changed into a Turkish city. Its churches had been converted into mosques; its citizens were followers of the Prophet of Mecca. Through the streets of this city our Grecian captives were conducted, until they reached a large mansion, which had, no doubt, once belonged to some aristocratic family, whose name had figured honorably on the annals of the Empire, but which, like most of the prominent edifices of the town, now possessed a Turkish owner. Into this dwelling Diogenes and his family were admittted; they were told that it would be at their disposal during their sojourn in the city, but that they should never leave it without the Turkish escort that had come with them from the shores of the Bosphorus. No other information was vouchsafed. Who the owner of the house was, or for what purpose they had been brought thither, they could not discover. They were kept carefully isolated from every communication with Greeks, and were forced to adopt a Turkish costume. They had no society but that of one another, and they never exchanged words with any one except the commander, who was the only person near them who spoke Greek. They had servants, and

Irene, her maid, but all these were persons whose language they could not understand. Whenever they left the house to enjoy the fresh air, Irene was forced to wear a veil, according to the fashion of the Turkish women. For the rest, they were well-treated, and they had all they desired. Their slightest wish seemed a law for the Turkish Commander.

CHAPTER VIII.

After the capture of Nicolaus, he had been conveyed to a subterranean dungeon. He would have been put to death immediately, but it was supposed that he held important secrets, which might be of use to the Greeks. The place where he lay chained, seemed to him a portion of that eternal prison, where the soul undergoes everlasting torture for its wickedness on earth. Not the faintest ray of light penetrated into that abode of perpetual gloom; no starless night was ever like unto it in blackness. Silence reigned profoundly; it was the silence of the tomb. Its walls that, for centuries, had been buried in the bosom of the earth, served as the foundation for an enormous tower, one of five that formed the Pentapyrgion, a prison for political offenders. Constantinople might fall to pieces with a sudden crash; no echo of the noise would reach the unfortunate inmate of that abode of death. There lay Nicolaus Lecapenos, the traitor to his Country and his God. While far from all that might distract, his mind vividly reverted to the past. He beheld, in the anguish of his soul, the mother who had endeavored to instil into his heart the seed of virtue, but whose wise counsels he had despised. There arose before him, one by one, the friends, in whose company he had begun to walk upon that road which finally led him to the unfortunate condition in which he now found himself. He saw so distinctly the day on which he first met Angela Ladrazzoni. She was then so young, so beautiful, and so innocent. Her guileless heart was beguiled by his deceitful tongue; he dragged her down to the lowest depths of misery. He saw Dimitrios and Irene; he remembered the fatal passion that had taken possession of him, which, a spark in the beginning, had become a mighty conflagration. He recalled to mind his treachery; he shrank back in terror from himself. A voice whispered, in the depths of his heart: "Nicolaus, return; raise thy heart, pray; it is never too late." Another spoke: "Too late, Nicolaus; too late forever. Thou hast forsaken God; thou hast followed Mahomet; let Mahomet help thee now." Suddenly, he shrieked, with a cry that seemed to pierce the very walls of his dungeon: "Oh, God! what is that? I see her," and he shrank back as far as he could into a corner of his prison. "She approaches; she is covered with blood; her eyes flash vengeance; her arm is uplifted to strike. Help! Mercy! Leila, pardon; spare me!" There was a heavy fall upon the ground; all was again silent as the tomb. Nicolaus had lost consciousness.

When he returned to his senses, the light was shining upon him; he lay on a couch in a small cell, the barred window of which admitted a few scanty rays of that benignant, though mysterious, force of nature, without which, life would become extinct upon the face of the earth. As Nicolaus opened his eyes, he looked bewildered around him; he knew not where he was. Had he exchanged one life for another, or was he still in the realm of mortality? Beside him stood a soldier. Nicolaus gazed upon him; his eyes met a countenance that he had seen somewhere he could not recall. Suddenly he turned and buried his face in the pillow; he had recognized the one who stood gazing at him.

"Dimitrios!" he moaned.

"I am Dimitrios, Nicolaus," the other replied. "I am here, not as an enemy, but to forgive. Remembering the example of our common Master, I am here to pardon—my bitterest enemy."

"My God! can it be possible?"

"Yes, it is possible. I pardon all, if thou wilt repent."

"Repent! How can there be repentance without mercy, and how can there be mercy for me?"

"There is mercy. Am I not merciful? and think you that God is less merciful than I?"

Nicolaus was silent. Dimitrios added:

"Pray; knock at the door of mercy. Will you promise me to pray?"

"I will endeavor."

Some days had passed since the scene we have just related.

The shock received by the nervous system of Nicolaus, had been so great, that he still lay prostrated in the cell where we left him. However, he was recovering.

He appeared much calmer, though from time to time a dark shadow would flit across his brow. Occasionally his lips seemed to move in prayer.

Dimitrios entered the room. Approaching the bedside of Nicolaus, he sat down. Taking the sick man's hand in his own, he said:

"Nicolaus, you are feeling better to-day; I think we may converse seriously. You have assured me, of your own accord, that you relinquish all claim to Irene. You also promised me that you would offer an explanation which would clear up the mystery of the last few days. Will you now fulfil your promise?

"Ah! my good friend," replied the sick man, "it is a bitter tale, but be it told to my own greater shame. You have now learned of my intimacy with the unfortunate Leila. When I conceived that fatal passion for Irene, I determined to ruin you, and to make Leila my tool. In order better to succeed, I made use of a third person. Michael Dorcas is a most intimate friend of John Diogenes; he is at present abroad, I believe. I caused him to meet Leila, as it were, accidentally. Obedient to my commands, she swore to him that she was affianced to you. Out of interest in his friend, he communicated this intelligence to him. This was the beginning of your sorrows. For more than two years I have been in secret communication with the Turks. On my last visit to Adrianople, Sultan Mohammed commanded me to return hither in disguise. In that disguise you have seen me. It was my pilgrim's garb that gained me admittance into the house of Diogenes. While at the Turkish fort, on the Bosphorus, I concocted the iniquitous plan that took Irene away. I determined to have her removed from Constantinople, and, by bribery, I gained over the Turkish Pasha to my cause. When I arrived in the city, everything worked even better than I had expected. I found Irene sick. I pretended to be a physician, and persuaded her father to remove her to the salubrious climate of Attica. To the Captain of a Greek vessel, with whom I was acquainted, I gave money to convey the family to Attica. Traitor, as ever, I discovered that the Captain carried despatches for the Doge of Venice, and this I found means to communicate to the Turks."

"But where is Irene?" asked Dimitrios, with impatience.

"Listen. The captain left Constantinople under the impression that he was bound for Athens. He was instructed to stop near the Turkish fort to take on board a detachment of soldiers who were to act ostensibly as the guard of Irene's family."

Dimitrios grew pale. Nicolaus continued:

"The soldiers had orders to allow the vessel to proceed no further than Thessalonica. Here they were to land the passengers."

"Great Heavens! Is Irene in the hands of the Turks? Oh, Nicolaus, it is monstrous—"

"Pardon me, my friend, did you not say that you forgave me all? It was wicked, cruel, barbarous, I hate myself for it, but be not alarmed."

Dimitrios buried his face in his hands and sobbed. "Continue," he moaned.

Nicolaus went on:

"On their arrival at Thessalonica, the soldiers had orders to conduct them to a mansion belonging to my friend, the Pasha; there they were to await me, and, meanwhile, to be treated with the greatest respect."

"And they are now in Thessalonica, and where?"

"Opposite the Church of the Twelve Apostles."

"I will go to them, I will save Irene."

"It would be rashness now."

"What then can we do?"

"I alone can save them. Had I my liberty! but, alas! I am condemned to die."

"What would you do?"

"After Constantinople falls, as it surely will, I would

go to Thessalonica, give them their freedom and return them to you."

"Can it not be done now?"

"Impossible. And besides, they are perfectly safe in Thessalonica, under the protection of the Pasha, while here they would be in the greatest danger."

"And if you die?"

"They will remain in the hands of the Turks."

"Nicolaus, did I expect no benefit from thee, even then would I endeavor to obtain thy life, but now a double motive impels me. Farewell!"

Dimitrios arose and departed.

The reader will easily surmise, that Nicolaus, having been found unconscious in his subterranean dungeon, had been transferred to a more agreeable prison, principally through the instrumentality of Dimitrios. The Emperor admired the youth's forgiving spirit, but he believed that justice should take its course, and he therefore refused to commute the sentence which condemned the traitor and murderer to death. The pleadings of Dimitrios had been in vain.

A half hour after the conversation with Nicolaus, Dimitrios had begged for an audience with the Emperor, to whose presence he was frequently admitted, not only by reason of the nobility of his birth, but, also, on account of the Monarch's affection toward him. On this occasion, however, he had long to wait. Finally the bearer of an imperial message approached him with a summons to the presence of his Majesty, into whose private apartments he was conducted. As he entered the room, the Emperor looked up, and Dimitrios noticed for the first time an expression of impatience on the Sovereign's face. The youth knelt before him, and the

Emperor, contrary to his custom, did not bid him rise. This appeared ominous to Dimitrios. Constantine thus addressed him:

"Dimitros, hast thou again come to disturb me in connection with that unfortunate renegade? Knowest thou not that weighty affairs of the Empire occupy all my attention?"

"Pardon me, your Majesty," Dimitrios replied, "if I have the boldness to intrude and encroach upon your valuable time, but I would now implore your clemency on my own behalf as well as that of a family most devoted to your interests and those of the Empire."

The Emperor's face assumed a softer expression, while a look of surprise overcast it as he enquired:

"What is it thou hast at heart, my son; hast thou transgressed a law, or hast thou been guilty of a breach of military discipline?"

"Neither, your Majesty, but my own happiness and that of persons most dear to me are in the hands of Nicolaus Lecapenos. His death will be the death stroke to that happiness."

The Emperor frowned.

"Explain thyself," he said.

Dimitrios in a few words related the occurrences of the past few days. The Emperor looked serious, perplexed, even sad. He shook his head as though an unpleasant duty lay before him.

"Dimitrios," he said, "what thou askest of me, may at first sight seem reasonable to thee. Gladly would I grant thy request, but reflect. There is here a question of the common good. The man whose life thou beggest me to spare, is a public malefactor. Had I alone been the victim of his crime, I would not hesitate an instant in exercising mercy, but he has shown himself an enemy of the Empire, yea, of society at large. My honor, the State, the people, eternal justice itself clamor loudly for his execution. Would I not be unfaithful to my trust, were I to let him live? Would it not be like harboring a venomous reptile who might give death to those who save its life?"

Dimitrios seemed crestfallen, the Emperor gazed at him with pity.

"Be brave," he spoke, "trust lovingly in Providence. I will reflect; if there is any possibility of saving the life of Nicolaus Lecapenos, thy request shall be granted. I will send thee word to thy dwelling before the hour of nine tomorrow; meanwhile, fare thee well!"

Dimitrios thanked the Sovereign, and, bowing profoundly before him, departed.

Leaving the Palace, he directed his steps toward the Augustaeum. For a long time he paced up and down, lost in reflection, and observing not that at a few paces distance, a stranger of rude appearance was intently gazing upon him. Suddenly he turned toward the Hippodrome, and the words of Diogenes seemed to ring in his ears: "On the twenty-fifth of next month, meet me at the Hippodrome."

"Where are they now?" he muttered. "Oh! Irene, Irene, had I wings, how gladly would I fly to thy assistance!"

These words had been uttered sufficiently loud to be understood by the stranger, on whose face, in spite of its stern and even cruel features, a look of deep compassion seemed to settle.

With a sigh, Dimitrios turned away toward the Church of St. Sophia. There at least he expected to find balm for his afflicted heart. Human aid had failed him, he would seek the Divine.

CHAPTER IX.

The execution of Nicolaus had been set for 10 o'clock of the day after the audience granted by the emperor to Dimitrios. The latter had visited the unfortunate prisoner to reconcile him, if possible, to his impending fate. He had found him resigned, though apparently downcast. Although our young Greek had lost all hope, still he endeavored to cheer the unfortunate man, by repeating to him the Emperor's promise to spare his life, if possible.

"Had I been able to communicate to them secrets which they supposed I had learned among the Turks, my life might have been spared, but I could give them no information; all I knew was the mission imposed upon me by the Sultan, and it is this very mission which becomes the principal reason for my execution, and which renders me dangerous to the Emperor."

Thus spoke the condemned man. In spite of the awful fate that awaited him, there was a lightness in his voice and a quickness in his eye which contrasted ill with his surroundings and the solemnity of the moment.

"Nicolaus, are you not afraid to die?" asked Dimitrios.

"Afraid to die? Not in the least. What is there to live for?"

As he pronounced these words, an image flashed before his mind; he seemed to behold Leila, as she stood before him in that fatal hour which was her last. Again he heard her voice, as she exclaimed: "What have I to live for?"

His countenance paled, he shuddered, his emotion seemed to give the lie to his words, but, regaining his self-control, he added:

"The only reason why I hope for life, the only motive why I cling to it, even though the black clouds of despair are fast rolling over me, is the earnest wish to give back Irene to you. I know that my death will separate her from you for ever."

O, God!" exclaimed Dimitrios, "is there no ray of hope to break the darkness of this night?"

All was darkness in his soul, life seemed a blank, happiness appeared to have departed out of it forever, and yet the star of faith was shining still, for Dimitrios was a firm believer in the governing hand of a wise Providence, without whose permission not a sparrow falls to the ground. Had this faith deserted him, he would have sunk down into the abyss of despair, his life would have become utterly wretched, but he believed, and his faith sustained him, it gave him hope, it made him feel that he would meet Irene again, if not in this world, then surely in a better one where pains and sorrow cease. It was his faith which, in all his woes, caused him to seek refuge in prayer, and which had rendered the Temple of St. Sophia so familiar to him. Grasping the hand of Nicolaus, he said:

"My good friend, all is not lost yet. I trust that the Emperor will be moved, he is naturally merciful, and I know that he loves me. Therefore, let us hope even in the midst of our darkness. I leave you now, but I feel that we shall meet again. I sincerely congratulate you on your return to God. The good priest who has shown himself so kind to you, will visit you again to-morrow morning, endeavor to persevere in your good dispositions."

A tear glistened in his eye, as he pressed the hand of the doomed man, and, with a heavy heart, he departed from the cell, gently closing the door behind him. Lost in sad reflections, he pursued his way until he reached the portal of his own home.

In one of the aristocratic quarters of the City of Constantine, stood a venerable mansion which had long been the dwelling of the ancestors of Dimitrios and Helena, who were the only survivors of the family. It was night when young Phocas passed through the arched doorway of his ancestral mansion. Going through a spacious courtyard, he entered a magnificently furnished room where a light was burning. On a rich couch, or lounge, as we might call it in our days, reclined the figure of a young girl. She had fallen asleep, but, as the footsteps of Dimitrios resounded on the tesselated pavement, she suddenly started from her gentle slumber. A gracious smile played upon her lips, as she welcomed the youth.

"Dimitrios," she spoke, "you have tarried long. I awaited with impatience your return, until, overcome with fatigue, my drooping eyelids refused to perform the nocturnal service I had demanded of them. But you appear sad, unusually depressed. Alas! I read upon your countenance that you have no favorable communication to make to me. Have you seen the Emperor?"

Dimitrios, seated beside his sister, related to her the events of the day, and closing his discourse, added:

"Still, I hope against hope, and put my trust in God, and He will not cause me to be tried above my strength."

With these words he arose and parted from Helena

for the night, both going to their respective apartments. The sister of Dimitrios Phocas was a tall girl, about three years his junior. Since the death of their mother, he had been to her more than a brother, he had taken the place of a father. She clung to him with all the ardor of her Southern heart, and looked up to him as to her only protector. His joys were hers, and she shared all his sorrows; there was not a pulsation of the heart of Dimitrios which did not find its echo in that of Helena. During the past few days he had communicated to her his afflictions, his fears and his hopes, and the only true consolation he derived outside of the supernatural strength which came to him from on High, he found in her society. She was as much like him in her character and in the noble aspirations of her soul, as she was in her features. In a word, for years she had been living his life, seeing with his eyes, hearing with his ears, thinking his thoughts, and feeling with his heart. Until now, no sorrow had ever darkened her path, and she had lived in blissful ignorance of that which bears the name of grief. She had been happy, because she saw Dimitrios happy, she loved Irene because Dimitrios loved her, for hers was not a jealous nature, and she willingly shared her brother's affection with one whom she looked upon as a sister. The first sorrow of her life had now cast its shadow over her young heart, and that sorrow was the same that wrapped the soul of Dimitrios in gloom. She retired to rest that night with an aching heart, for she knew that her brother was suffering and she could do nothing to alleviate his pain. Intense anxiety for the fate of Irene, dread and uncertainty, and the horrible fear that Nicolaus would be executed kept her awake for the rest of the night.

Slowly the hours dragged along, the night had never seemed so interminable. Thus far, she had never known what sleeplessness was, but now she sought in vain for that refreshing gift of nature which is always welcome to the sufferer and the weary, but it came not.

Dimitrios, too, tossed restlessly upon his couch. With longing, and yet with fear, he awaited the dawn of that day which was to decide his fate, and when Aurora began to gild the eastern sky, and the first glimmering of the new-born day appeared within his room, his heart beat rapidly, as though the sentence of death were to be executed upon himself. Fatigued, he arose from his couch. His first thoughts ascended to the Author of life, and, casting himself upon his knees, he spent some time in silent prayer. Arising, he left the apartment and went out to the inner court. How delicious was the morning! The fresh breeze from the harbor wafted the perfume of many flowers upon the fragrant air, the light spray of the fountain sprinkled the face of Dimitrios, who had seated himself beside it, while a captive bird raised its melodious voice to greet the advent of another day. All seemed so out of harmony with the soul of the young man, where night still reigned and no ray had yet announced the advent of a joyous morning. Nature appeared to sport with his sorrows.

The Emperor had promised to send him word to his dwelling, hence Dimitrios decided not to leave his house until all hope had entirely vanished. Helena had also come out to seek refreshment in the cool air of the morning, and she now sat beside her brother. They were silent, for no words seemed adequate to convey their emotions, which were better felt than expressed. The hours had passed slowly, and the warm rays of the sun forced the youthful pair to withdraw into the house. Dimitrios was evidently in a state of agitation, and he paced to and fro, occasionally stopping to listen, as a distant sound broke upon his ear. Helena respected the deep sorrow of her brother, and spoke not, though the look she occasionally cast upon him, betokened her anxiety.

The hours passed, and yet no word from the Emperor. The shadow on the dial indicated that in another half hour the moment of the execution would have arrived. The heart of Dimitrios beat almost audibly, every moment he would stand and listen. Silence itself had now become unbearable, his agitated thoughts sought vent. Turning to Helena, he exclaimed:

"My dear sister, I fear the worst. If there had been a favorable decision, I would have heard of it ere now. Only a few minutes more, and all will be over."

"Lose not hope, dear brother, perhaps the Emperor may have delayed the execution in order to gain time for reflection. It appears to me that the very fact of your receiving no tidings is good news, it shows that, thus far, nothing has transpired."

"On the contrary, Helena, I will not receive information if the execution takes place. The Emperor wishes to spare himself all further importunities, and, when the head of Nicolaus shall have fallen, he will endeavor to console me. Alas! poor, unfortunate man, is this the end of one whom I once supposed to be my friend! Do we not behold clearly that the wages of sin is death? But I have now no time to moralize, every nerve in my body trembles, my heart appears as if ready to burst out of my breast, my blood is on fire. O! Helena; Helena! suspense is worse than death. Suspense, do I say? No, there is no longer suspense, but certainty, dreadful, inexorable certainty stares me in the face. The hour is passed, behold the shadow moves onward in its course. Alas! Nicolaus Lecapenos is no more! His soul has passed through the dark valley of the shadows of death, it has heard its sentence. And thou, Irene, the light of my life, yea, my life itself, thou art lost to me, lost forever. The coldness of the grave benumbs me, its shadow is cast over me, why should I live? O, Constantine, Constantine, thou last scion of the house of Paleologos! is this thy affection? Where are thy words of esteem? Scattered by the wind of thy actions. Where is my love for thee? Dashed to pieces against the rocks of a stern reality. O! what cruel destiny is mine! My God! my God! strengthen me lest I sink forever in this shoreless and unfathomable ocean of dire anguish. Lord, Lord, save me, for I perish!"

A violent storm had burst. Dimitrios fell exhausted upon a couch, he buried his face in a cushion, the strong man sobbed aloud, his frame shook violently.

"Brother, brother," exclaimed Helena, alarmed, running towards Dimitrios and throwing her arms around him. "Brother, calm your emotion, do not give yourself thus over to your feelings. Be brave, have you thus entirely succumbed to weakness?"

"Pardon, my sister, my too long pent up feelings need vent."

"Hark, Dimitrios, I hear footsteps."

The young man started up and ran towards the door. On the threshold he was met by a member of the Imperial Guards, who, in few words, informed him that his presence was desired at the Palace. Hastily taking leave of his sister, and carelessly throwing his mantle over his shoulders, he hurried to the street, and, almost running, he directed his course toward the enclosure, where the Palace stood.

On appearing before the Emperor, he noticed that there was a look of disappointment and displeasure upon his countenance. On bidding Dimitrios arise, he spoke:

"My son, we have once more been deceived in Nicolaus."

"Is Nicolaus still alive, Sire?"

"He is, my dear boy, but he ought not to be."

Dimitrios gazed in mute astonishment. The Emperor continued:

"After long and painful reflection, and a formidable struggle between justice and mercy, I finally decided that the victory should belong to the latter."

Dimitrios breathed more freely.

"Imagine my consternation when I learned that this morning the cell of the prisoner was found vacant; the door had been left open, and both Nicolaus and his jailer had disappeared. Search was made for them in all directions, but it has proved useless. The traitor has escaped."

"It is a mystery, your Majesty, a mystery which may be cleared up in time."

"Dimitrios, if you assist in solving the mystery, I will be your debtor. Morosini will lend you all assistance. As for those who are dear to you, I will endeavor to mature some plan for their deliverance. Meanwhile be of good cheer. You may now depart."

Dimitrios left the presence of his Imperial Majesty with a lighter heart than when he had entered the Palace. He felt relieved now that he knew that Nicolaus was still alive. He could not suspect him of treachery. He had escaped merely to save his own life and to rescue Irene. Even now he was, perhaps, on his way to Thessalonica to save Diogenes and his children. The guileless youth had not yet learned to fathom the almost unfathomable depths of a hypocrite's heart.

CHAPTER X.

"You have had a most narrow escape, Nicolaus," said a cut-throat kind of a man, seated in a small house situated in one of the many tortuous streets of the city. Observe him attentively, and you will recognize the individual who stood gazing at Dimitrios on the Augustaeum, on the evening of his disappointing audience with the Emperor. Opposite him sat a person whom no power on earth could have recognized as Nicolaus Lecapenos. He was clad in the garb of the lowest classes of the population, while his unkempt hair and beard, both of an almost fiery red, seemed to indicate that he was a descendant of the Germanic nations of the North. His brow was furrowed, while his nose and cheeks resembled three glowing coals.

"You speak the truth this time, Fortuny," replied Nicolaus, "for, the first time in your life, your Catalan tongue has not told a lie."

Fortuny, brandishing a large knife of Toledo workmanship, retorted:

"Did I not know you were jesting, Nicolaus, this blade would quench its thirst in your blood, and you would find that it is less easy to escape from a son of Catalonia than from Constantine Paleologos; but, leave all jokes aside, and relate to me the manner of your escape. First, however, take a good draught out of this skin. It contains an excellent red wine, made in Castile. I obtained it not long since on board a vessel from Barcelona."

Hereupon, Fortuny handed the goat-skin to Nicolaus, who, after a copious draught, returned it to the owner, the latter glueing his lips to the mouth of the vessel and imbibing freely, as he said, in honor of the escape of the Greek.

"Now, old friend," he added, "begin your story."

"You must know," said Nicolaus. "that the brutes threw me into a black hole, under one of the five towers of the Pentapyrgion. I thought my time had come, and that I was about to be left there as food for the rats. By all the gods of Olympus, if there is a place on earth resembling hell, it is that dungeon. I assure you that, when a man is left all to himself in a Tartarean vault like that, he sees strange sights. Balls of fire seemed to dance before my eyes; phantasmata of the imagination became realities. What happened after that I cannot tell, for I must have fainted. The next thing I knew was, that I lay on a couch in a cell, and, who do you think was bending over me? Really, it seems like a dream. Dimitrios Phocas was there. Noble youth! I hated him once, but it is impossible to do so longer. He forgave me all, he said. He exerted himself to the utmost to save my life. Now, Fortuny, I am a bad man, but bad as I am, I cannot longer hate Dimitrios. It is true, I deceived him. I made him believe that I was repentant, but, notwithstanding this, I esteem him now, and will do for him all that I can, but one thing—I cannot give up Irene. To come to the point: Constantine was inexorable, and it is fortunate that he was, or I would not be here. He flattered Dimitrios with vain hopes, but, as sure as you are alive, I would, ere this, have crossed the Styx, had not fortune favored me. My jailer happened to be an enemy of the house of Paleologos; I soon discovered this. Moreover, I found out that there was one idol the fellow worshiped with all the intensity of his heart—gold. For the glittering metal he would, at any time, be willing to sell his soul. I put a handful of gold pieces into his hand. I promised that, after the fall of the city, I would make his fortune. The old fool's head was turned; the gold dazzled him. He obtained for me a disguise: a suit of clothes belonging to one of the workmen of the prison. In the middle of the night I left my cell. Knowing the entire place, he conducted me to an exit where, fortunately for us, the guard had fallen asleep. My jailer, who was a boon companion to many of the soldiers, had, beforehand, taken the precaution to dose, with an intoxicating beverage, the poor fellow, whom he knew would be on duty on this spot, and at this hour. The potion worked admirably. To these fortunate circumstances I owe my escape. I have placed my jailer in safety, where he may remain concealed until after the city capitulates, or it is taken."

"And now, Nicolaus, what are your plans?"

"Plans? Well, I know them not myself. Have I not the Sultan's orders to remain in Constantinople until it is captured?"

"Do you intend to abide by these orders?"

"What else can I do?"

"But your life is in danger."

"I am aware of the fact; but you see, old man, I am now between Scylla and Charybdis. At all events, I want you to help me in a matter of great importance. Here is your reward."

Nicolaus held a small bag of gold coins before the greedy eyes of the Catalan.

"You know that John Diogenes and his family are held in custody at Thessalonica. I am uneasy concerning them, for it has been impossible for me to receive any news of their condition. I wish you to go thither, for you have more than enough opportunities at your disposal, find out how they fare, and report to me."

"Give me the gold first."

"No! No! That would never do. You know I do not pay in advance. Fulfil your mission, and this gold is yours."

The Spaniard hesitated. The journey was tedious, and not without danger; on the other hand, an opportunity to gain such a sum of money was not to be lost.

"Will you agree?" asked Nicolaus.

Fortuny made no reply.

"Well, if you will not, I know others who would be well pleased with half this sum. Farewell!"

Nicolaus arose, as if about to depart.

"Hold!" cried the Catalan, "when do you wish me to start?"

"This very night."

"The time is short."

"Yes; but the affair is urgent."

"Well, Nicolaus, you may rely on me. I will leave to-night by a vessel, the owner of which is my friend. Without delay, I will return."

"Well said, but, ere you depart, I must ask some information of you. What news is there of the Sultan's movements? Has he left Adrianople?"

"I have some wonderful news. The army and the fleet are fast encircling the doomed city, and the Sultan has placed himself at the head of his troops. The Bosphorus is filled with Turkish ships. You remember

that immense brass cannon that was cast at Adrianople?
It is calculated that it will throw a stone of six hundred pounds' weight. Well, two months ago, it started on its journey for Constantinople, and only a few days since it arrived at the army, amid the acclamations of the multitude. In a day or two, I have no doubt, it will be placed in position, ready to belch forth death and destruction over this unfortunate city. The strength of the Turkish forces is of three hundred thousand men, against which the handful of Greeks and Genoese that Constantine commands, can avail nothing."

"So we may expect the siege to begin at any moment?"

"Yes, at any moment."

"Well, Fortuny, in a few days I hope we shall meet again. I will rely on your prudence and intrepidity. Farewell."

Nicolaus now arose, pressed the hand of the Catalan, and departed.

A few hours later, Fortuny had left the city.

Meanwhile neither the Emperor, Dimitrios, nor Morosini, were enabled to form any conjectures concerning the whereabouts of Nicolaus. The Emperor had, after his interview with Dimitrios, returned to the Palace of Blachernae, in the suburb of that name, which, since the twelfth century, had gradually superseded the old Palace as an imperial residence. However, the latter had not been entirely abandoned, and it was within its walls that Dimitrios had conversed with his sovereign on the occasions mentioned in the preceding chapters.

On the morning after the departure of Fortuny, Morosini and Dimitrios met accidentally on the *Mese*, or Middle street, in one of the *emboli*, or arcades, which lined it on the sides.

"Well, dear boy," said Morosini, with a serious countenance, "are you ready? You will soon hear the call to arms. The Turkish army may be seen from the towers. Multitudes cover the land on all sides. The gates in the Theodosian walls have all been closed, and the bridges over the ditch which connect them with the country roads, have been taken down, so that Constantinople is now cut off from communication with the outer world, and it must depend upon itself. Do you hear that? It is the sound of the bugle, calling on every defender of the city to join his regiment. The Emperor is at Blachernae, but you may be sure that he will be everywhere, for Constantine is a brave Prince. Return to the *Chalce*, where your quarters are, for you will be needed. Be a brave man, Dimitrios, and remember, that you are the descendant of an Emperor, and a hero, the courageous old Nicephorus Phocas. You may not save the Empire, but, at least, the honor of defending it is yours. But, tell me, where is Helena?"

"My poor Helena!" sighed Dimitrios, "she is at home. She fears much for my safety, and her alarm nearly distracts her. Morosini, my friend, if I should fall, will you be a protector to my sister?"

"Dimitrios, I swear to you, that as long as there is life in Vincent Morosini, as long as his heart beats, as long as one drop of blood courses through his veins, no harm shall come to Helena; do you believe me?"

"Ah! my dear, good, noble friend, it is so much like yourself. Thanks, a thousand thanks!"

Dimitrios pressed warmly the hand of his friend.

"Now, Dimitrios," said Morosini, "I must leave you, but we shall frequently be together. The city may be in the possession of the Greeks only for a short time longer. At the first opportunity we shall procure horses and ride through Constantinople, to study its streets and fortifications, and thus to bid it a last farewell. I will meet you soon again."

The two friends parted, the former going to the quarters of the Emperor's Guards, and the latter towards the Golden Horn.

When, on the morrow, the sun arose over Constantinople, it was to cast its rays upon the Turkish army encamped outside of the walls. The instruments of mediæval warfare mingled with those of modern times, which were still in a rude condition. Huge towers and battering rams arose at intervals in the enemy's encampment, while catapults stood ready to hurl deadly missiles into the city. Instruments such as these had frequently been tried upon the walls of impregnable Constantinople, though unsuccessfully, but Mahomet had other offensive weapons to rely on, weapons, to resist which, those walls had not been built. It was more than a century, since for the first time, the roar of artillery had been heard above the din of battle. At Cressy, in 1346, it had been used by the English against the French. Although more than a hundred years had elapsed since then, the use of gunpowder had made comparatively little progress, and small firearms were only beginning to be employed. Large cannon, however, were used extensively. The artillery of Mahomet consisted of fourteen powerful batteries, which were directed against the city from the land side.

The defenders of Constantinople were not idle. Detachments of soldiers were stationed on the terraces between the wall of Constantine and that of Theodosius, while the mouths of cannon were pointed towards

the enemy. From the tower in Galata, on the other side
of the Golden Horn, an iron chain was stretched across
the harbor and attached to the Tower of Eugenius, in
Constantinople. The entrance to the harbor was also
guarded by the Greek ships. The dying Byzantine Empire determined to sell its life dearly. The Emperor
himself assumed command of his forces, while the Genoese, Giustiniani, was second to him.

While all Constantinople remained in expectation of
the things to come, Dimitrios Phocas, and many of his
comrades, were stationed at the Palace of Blachernae,
they being held in reserve. The ardent nature of the
young man could ill brook the state of inactivity to
which he was condemned, while so many soldiers of the
Empire stood at the post of danger on the ramparts, but
Morosini sustained his courage and cheered him with
the assurance that he would soon be called upon to take
an active part in the defense of his native city. While
they were conversing on the possibilities and probabili-
ties of the siege, suddenly loud peals, as of thunder,
rent the air. Both men understood the meaning of the
sound; they rushed to the walls, whence a sight of the
Turkish camp might be obtained; the air was filled with
smoke. For a short while there was silence; then, while
they gazed towards the Moslem army, white clouds suddenly burst forth from the enemy's ranks, all along the
line, and, after a brief interval, another prolonged roar
re-echoed over the surrounding country; Mahomet had
brought his fourteen batteries to bear upon Constantinople at the same time. Almost immediately the noise
of artillery resounded from over the sea. The Turkish
ships were playing upon the city, while a naval combat
was taking place between the Greeks and Turks. The

roar became deafening, for the Greeks on the walls had opened fire on their enemies, and formidable engines of war on both sides were belching forth deadly fire, which cost many a life.

In solemn silence Morosini and Dimitrios contemplated the deadly conflict. The ardent Greek would gladly have cast himself into the fray, but military discipline held him aloof, and condemned him to play the part of an idle spectator. In the midst of the excitement, his thoughts wandered away now to Helena, whom he had entrusted to the care of a faithful old servant, and whose fright he painfully pictured to himself, as the sound of artillery broke upon her ear, then to Irene. As the image of the latter flitted across his mind, a feeling of unutterable anxiety filled his heart. Where can she be? Perhaps, at this very moment—Oh! he dared not think of it—in the power of a cruel follower of Mahomet. And where is Nicolaus? These painful thoughts filled his mind, as the deafening roar of cannon sent forth its echoes.

While the two friends stood silently gazing at the awful scene, an artillery soldier passed them.

"What is the progress of affairs, friend?" asked Dimitrios.

"Bad enough!" replied the soldier. "Pieces of the wall are falling; it was not built to withstand gunpowder. Moreover, what is still worse, the walls are too narrow for our cannon, and the recoil shakes them to an alarming extent, we fear lest we may have to desist firing."

"In that case," exclaimed Dimitrios, "Heaven protect us. we will be at the mercy of our enemies."

"It is not so bad as that, yet," said Morosini; "we shall fight desperately."

"But what can we do without cannon?"

"If a breach is made, we shall defend it to the last man, and if the Turks enter, it will not be before hundreds of the infidels shall have fallen under our blows."

As Morosini, who was now clad in full armor, spoke these words, he grasped the hilt of his sword, as if to add weight to his assertion.

Meanwhile, the roar of cannon continued; clouds of smoke filled the air, and the work of death went on; the agony of Byzantium had begun.

CHAPTER XI.

The siege had been lasting five days, sometimes the cannon roaring without intermission for several hours, while at intervals the bombardment ceased, to begin with renewed vigor. On the morning of the sixth day, Dimitrios, being free from duty, was, according to agreement, met by Morosini at the palace of Blachernae. The latter had procured two beautiful and richly caparisoned horses. As they both stood beside the animals, ready to mount them, Morosini spoke:

"Dimitrios, you are acquainted with the political and religious history of your country, I know; but, although you are a Constantinopolitan by birth, and I am a foreigner, nevertheless, I pride myself in knowing Constantinople better than you do. You will, therefore, not take it amiss if I assume the role of an instructor."

"By no means, my dearest friend; on the contrary, my gratitude to you for this, as well as for all else, will be unbounded."

"Well, let us begin here. Since the twelfth century the old imperial palace has been gradually abandoned for this one in the suburb of Blachernae. I doubt whether the Emperors have done wisely. The old palace, connected with so many endearing traditions, is so beautifully situated on the Bosphorus; would it not have been better to keep it in a good condition of repair, instead of allowing it to go to ruin? But, such is the nature of man. Yonder you behold the dungeon of the Pentapyrgion, from which the traitor, Nicolaus, so recently escaped. I believe that you had never set foot within its walls until you visited the unfortunate man."

"You are right. I had often wondered what the interior of the Pentapyrgion was like, but I had never seen it."

Both the young men sprang into their saddles, and as they trotted on, Morosini continued:

"Yonder, to the northeast, you behold the church of St. Mary of Blachernae. Have you ever been within it?"

"Yes, once; I assisted at the Eucharistic Sacrifice on the feast of St. Spiridion."

"Do you behold yonder hill? It is the Cosmidion. It was there that the first Crusaders pitched their tents during the reign of Alexius Comnenus."

"Yes; I have read with the greatest interest that portion of our history in the works of the celebrated female historian, **Anna Comnena**, the daughter of the Emperor Alexius."

"Now allow me to draw your attention to the walls. That with the massive towers, at the extreme northwestern portion of the city, and to our left, is the wall of Heraclius, built in the seventh century. It protects the palace and the suburb of Blachernae. The walls of Constantinople have all been erected at various epochs and under different Emperors. The old Megarian city of Byzantium stood at the extreme eastern portion of Constantinople, there where now are the palace, St. Sophia, the Hippodrome and adjacent buildings. The first Christian Emperor designed to erect his New Rome on seven hills like its namesake in the West. This plan was executed, but only long after his death. The original walls of Constantine stretched on the south along the Propontis to the mouth of the River Lycus and, on the north, along the Golden Horn to the Church of the Saviour, which lies yonder to the southeast. Both these walls Constantine united by the land wall passing around the Polyandrion, near the Church of the Holy Apostles. The two Theodosian walls were erected early in the fifth century during the reign of Theodosius II. The town gates in the latter walls, which are now closed on account of the siege, correspond with the seven gates in the wall of Constantine. The Leontine wall was constructed during the reign of Leo the Armenian in the Ninth Century. Thus, you see, the city is fortified first by the great ditch, then by the Theodosian walls back of it, the wall of Heraclius, the Leontine wall and finally the wall of Constantine, which is the oldest and which forms the inner line. Now let us return and follow the land wall."

"We are in a dangerous position," said Dimitrios, "entirely exposed to the enemy's fire."

"It is dangerous everywhere," answered Morosini, "let us trust in the protection of our guardian angels. On the other hand, keep your eyes open, you can hear the balls as they fly, and see them some time before they fall, so that we may evade them. We have six gates to pass, among them that of Polyandrion which opens on the road to Adrianople, the Roussion, the gate of the Heptapyrgion, near the Castle of the Seven Towers, and the Golden gate. The last named is nearly at the extreme end of the wall towards the Propontis."

Thus conversing, while an occasional ball would fly over their heads, strike the walls or tear up the earth of the terraces, the two friends rode along the fortifications, until with mutual agreement they put spurs to their horses and galloped at full speed, until they had reached the southwestern angle of the city, where the waters of the Propontis or Sea of Marmora wash the walls of Constantinople, then, turning to the left, they followed the sea wall until they reached the harbor of Theodosius, the mouth of which was protected by two towers which had recently been joined by a wall. There they turned to the left and rode in the direction of the Polyandrion, where, by the gate of that name, they entered the older portion of the city of Constantine. Riding in a southeasterly direction, they reached the Forum of Theodosius, passing near the aqueduct of Valens, and the Church of the Pantocrator, in the Monastery, attached to which, as Morosini pointed out to Dimitrios, the Latins had had their headquarters in the preceding century. Proceeding still further east, they finally arrived at the ancient Acropolis, with which we have been rendered familiar as being the spot near which St. Sophia stands. After some rest and refreshment taken in the quarters of the Imperial Guards at the old palace and a brief visit to St. Sophia, the two friends again mounted their horses, and, passing along the shores of the Golden Horn, proceeded as far as the gate Xylocircus, whence they returned to the Blachernae palace. They had thus completed the circuit of the city, with the exception of the space between the harbor of Theodosius and the Acropolis, which they had omitted, by taking the route we have indicated past the Polyandrion. Morosini had pointed out many points of inferior interest which were unknown to Dimitrios, and the latter expressed himself as perfectly satisfied.

The day was now nearly spent, and out towards the west the spears of the Turkish soldiery glittered in the mellow rays of the sun as it descended towards the horizon, while the report of their cannon reminded the frightened inhabitants of Constantinople that the enemy was before the walls. The clouds in the west gradually lost their topaz hue, till, as so many tongues of fire, they shot across the skies, slowly mellowing into darkness. Sombre, and still more sombre, grew the shadows on the earth, the blue green of the plains becoming purple. The gorgeous tints of the sunset vanished, as the ever deepening shades announced the coming of the night. By degrees a melancholy pall was cast by nature's hand over the beleagured city, fit emblem of the dark clouds of apprehension that hovered over the hearts of its inhabitants. The reports of Turkish cannon grew less frequent, until they finally ceased, leaving in their stead a painful silence that hung heavily over the population.

Some hours had passed since Dimitrios and Morosini had returned from their excursion, and the Greek youth had hastened homeward to his sister. He found her alone and lost in revery.

"O! brother," she exclaimed, as she saw him enter, "how long this day has seemed! It appeared as though you would never come. Fearful apprehensions filled my mind; I saw you standing on the walls, and, as the continuous roar of the cannon sounded in my ears, I imagined those deadly balls flying around you—and, oh!"

The affrighted girl bent her head over her arm that was leaning on a table near by. After a brief silence she continued:

"My imagination was so strong, it worked so fearfully.

I saw you struck by one of those frightful messengers of death. I saw you fall."

The poor girl burst into tears and sobbed aloud, moaning:

"O! Dimitrios, it is awful."

"Calm your fears, my sister," the youth replied, "thus far I have not been called upon to perform active duty."

"But, Dimitrios, you will have to bear your portion of the labor and share in the great struggle; brother, my poor brother, I can stand it no longer. Expose not your life; there are enough soldiers without you, one more or less will not cause the city to succumb. Remember you are the only one left me; what? O! what shall I do without you; what will become of me if you fall?"

The heart of Dimitrios bled, he could find no reply.

"Speak, brother, speak. Will you remain with your sister, and not leave her again?"

"But, my dearest Helena, in defending Constantinople I am defending you. Of what use can I be to you in the house? Pray do not dissuade me."

"O! No, no, no! You are risking your life, they will kill you; Dimitrios, you must not, shall not go. By all that is dear to us, by the memory of our departed father, by the love of our mother, I beseech you, stay."

Dimitrios felt his heart yielding even against the dictates of his judgment, but, making a superhuman effort, he said:

"Helena, would you wish me to shrink from the fulfillment of a sacred duty? If my father were alive, he would stand beside his son to join in the glorious combat against the infidel, my mother herself would gird the sword around me. Would you have it said that a descendant of Nicephorus Phocas has shown himself a coward? Did you not often read to me how, in the tenth century, our glorious ancestor was the terror of the Saracens? Shall I be unworthy of the conqueror of Aleppo? Are not the bronze gates of Adana, Mopsuestia and Tarsus the trophies of his victory? And think, Helena, how many helpless orphans there are, how many widowed mothers, how many tender maidens, who hold out their hands imploringly to me, crying: Dimitrios Phocas, help us, save us from the Turks. And shall I turn a deaf ear to their supplications, shall I abandon them to their fate?"

Helena gazed at the inspired youth with admiration. In spite of her grief she could not help sharing his enthusiasm.

"Dimitrios," she exclaimed, "you are a noble boy; yes, you are made of the stuff of which heroes are made. My heart is bleeding, breaking, dying, but, my brother, I give you up for the love of our country and of our God. Go! Fight, conquer or die, and if you fall, your sister will not survive you. The same grave shall contain the bodies of Dimitrios and Helena."

Dimitrios caught the girl in his arms and pressed her to his heart.

"You speak as a true daughter of Byzantium should speak, Helena. My mother, noble woman! lives again —you are her image, my sister."

Seating himself beside her, he continued:

"Now, that you are calm, I will break to you a piece of news which I dared not mention until I knew that you were ready to make a sacrifice. Now listen, my brave heroine. The Emperor has decided to make a sortie to-morrow, and to lead it in person. The Sultan's batteries are playing havoc with the walls, and, above all, one of his cannon performs deadly work. Our brave Emperor is determined to beard the lion in his den and, if possible, take the battery and spike the cannon. He will leave the city under cover of night, and, before the morning dawns, we shall be hand to hand with the accursed brutes."

"What do you say, Dimitrios, we? Are you going?"

"My sister, did you not tell me to be a hero; do you retract?"

"No, Dimitrios," moaned the sobbing girl. "No! but it is awful, I fear to lose you," and she clung to him as though they were taking him away from her by force, while she buried her face on his shoulder. "Must you go? Has the Emperor lost his senses? Does he not know that his handful of men cannot stand against the hordes of barbarians?"

"The case is desperate, Helena, we must risk it. I feel for you, sister. Were I alone, O! how gladly, and with what alacrity, would I cast myself into the midst of our foes! But my heart sinks within me, it is crushed, when I think of you. But duty calls, stern duty summons me to its side, and when duty calls, we must obey. Pray for me, and, like Moses on the mountain, raise your hands to heaven, while I struggle against the enemies of Christ. Now, Helena, dear, I must be gone. The night is already advanced. I must join the ranks. I must hasten."

The poor girl threw her arms around her brother's neck and sobbed:

"Dimitrios, my dear, dear brother, do not leave me. What shall I do without you?"

"Be strong, Helena. Trust in God."

"The spirit is willing, brother, but the flesh is weak, but I resign myself to God's holy will."

The suffering girl cast herself upon her knees, and with her eyes and hands raised to heaven, and tears streaming down her cheeks, she exclaimed:

"Not my will, Father, but thine be done!"

The scene was heartrending; many a stern soul would have been melted on beholding it, and the reader may well imagine what the heart of Dimitrios must have felt.

"Helena," he exclaimed, "let us unite our sacrifice for God and our country."

He fell upon his knees, and with eyes raised heavenward, prayed:

"Eternal God, who didst command Abraham to sacrifice his son Isaac, help us in this hour of trial. Thou dost require of us a sacrifice, from which human nature shrinks in terror, but Thou who didst strengthen the Father of the faithful, hear our prayer, that grace may conquer in our hearts. I offer to Thee, Heavenly Father, the sacrifice of my life, and of that which is even dearer to me than life, of my only sister, in honor of the great Sacrifice of Calvary. Cross of my Redeemer, be my strength in the midst of my tribulation."

Dimitrios arose. He seemed another man. Helena, too, had grown calmer, firm determination showed itself upon her face.

"I go, Helena, at the call of duty. If the sacrifice of my life is demanded, my dearest friend will provide for you. You know him; Morosini will be your brother."

Brother and sister embraced each other, and the dreadful ordeal was over. Dimitrios was gone. Helena stood gazing at the door through which he had passed, as though she still beheld his form. Then a comprehension of her utter loneliness burst upon her, she cast herself upon the couch, and sobbed aloud.

"O, why did I let him go?" she said. "Dimitrios, my brother, shall I ever see you again, shall my eyes once more rest upon your manly face, shall I press your hand again, shall I ever read to you, as I did in those happy days, now past forever? Alas! is there happiness on earth?"

A voice sounded within the depths of her soul:

"The life of man upon earth is a warfare. . . . Man born of a woman, living for a short time, is filled with many miseries."

"It is true!" she exclaimed. "I had often read those passages of Job, but never did I understand them until now. My life had always been so tranquil, so undisturbed, but now the warfare has begun. I must bear my cross as others have borne theirs, but the cross leads to eternal life. Patience, my soul, after this life follows another, where the weary soul finds rest and we part no more."

CHAPTER XII.

The night was dark; not a star shone in the firmament. The Emperor could not have chosen a better time for the execution of his plans. The Turks were still at a considerable distance from the city, and it was deemed necessary that the sortie should be made at an early hour of the morning, in order that the unsuspecting enemy should be met before daybreak. The Emperor had decided to lead in person the attack, proceeding from the gate of Charisius, while the Genoese Giustiniani would head another from the Selymbria gate. Each would command a thousand men, attack separate batteries, but, if necessary, concentrate their forces on the great battery, where stood the famous cannon from Adrianople. The Emperor had been advised not to make the attempt, on account of the great distance of the Turkish army, and the difficulty there would be in effecting a retreat without severe loss in case of failure, but the thought of the incalculable damage that was being wrought by the enemy's cannon, decided him to attempt the hazardous enterprise. Only the infantry were to form the detachments. These were armed with crossbows, in imitation of the Crusaders, a rude species of small firearms that were just coming into use, spears and ponderous swords.

Both detachments were, at an early hour of the morning, drawn up behind their respective gates. The entire affair had been managed with so much secrecy, that most of the inhabitants of Constantinople were ignorant of what was taking place. At the appointed hour, and, at a given sign, both gates were simultaneously opened, and the troops marched out. The vanguard was formed by those who carried firearms; these were followed by the men with the crossbows; then came the light infantry with lances and swords. The rear was brought up by the Varangian Guards, among whom rode the Emperor. Dimitrios was there in full armor, with cuirass, helmet and sword. On his breastplate was blazoned the ancient device of Byzantium, the crescent and the star.

In perfect silence, and as noiselessly as their numbers would permit, marched the columns. Stillness reigned supremely; not a sound was wafted upon the restful air. There was absolutely nothing to indicate the presence of an invading army. Suddenly a flash of lightning shot athwart the sky; it was momentary, but sufficient to render visible all surrounding objects. To the eyes of the astounded Greeks, it showed the Turkish tents. They lay there in peaceful silence, indicating naught of the savage hearts with their fierce passions that were beating beneath them. A sound of distant thunder rolled under the vault of heaven, a sign of the coming storm. Simultaneously with the ominous sound from the heavens, a flash of light suddenly burst forth from the Turkish camp; it was followed by a loud report.

"We are discovered!" exclaimed the Emperor; then turning to one of his staff, he gave orders to halt. The bugle-sound re-echoed in the stillness of the night; it was repeated from a distance towards the south: the answer from Giustiniani's columns. At the same moment there was another flash, followed by a report, and a ball flew whistling over the heads of the soldiers. The lightning flashed, showing the Turkish camp, which had now become like a beehive, teeming with life and activity. The Emperor, turning towards two of the highest officers in the army, who stood beside him, asked their advice.

"Sire," replied the elder of the two, a veteran soldier, "it would be madness to continue. It would be worse than attacking Mahomet's forces in broad daylight. Besides the danger of being mowed down by their cannon before reaching them, in this darkness we would be unable to distinguish friend from foe. My advice is, that we retreat."

"And I will act upon it," said the Emperor; "we can ill afford to sacrifice our men uselessly."

The bugle sounded the retreat, and the columns wheeled around, returning in an inverse order from which they had come, the Imperial Guards taking the lead, and the men with the firearms bringing up the rear. Again the lightning flashed; again a report was heard, and another ball flew whistling through the air. The light from the heavens had shown the Turks that the Greeks were in full retreat. A cry that rent the air, arose from their ranks:

"God is God, and Mahomet is His Prophet!"

The bugle sounded the double-quick step and the Grecian columns ran in perfect order toward the city, while the Turkish-cannon balls flew thick and fast over them. Fortunately, the enemy aimed too high. The gates were reached and closed; the expedition had aborted. The companies were disbanded, the Imperial Guards returning to their quarters, where, before they were dismissed, the roll was called. As each one was named, the answer came:

"I am here."

The list of names had been nearly read, all those called being present. Finally, the officer's voice sounded:

"Dimitrios Phocas!"

There was no reply. The soldiers gazed at one another in mute astonishment; there was one man missing, and that one Dimitrios.

Although he had been only a short time in the service, he had grown to be a universal favorite, nor was any one so much esteemed among the Guards as he.

It was also known how high he stood in the Emperor's estimation, and how closely he was linked by the ties of friendship to the Emperor's Italian favorite, Morosini. This added no little to the universal esteem in which he was held. It fell, consequently, like a thunderbolt upon the soldiers when there was no answer to the call of his name. Dimitrios had never been known to have been guilty of a breach of discipline, and it could not be supposed that his absence was voluntary, therefore, some accident must have befallen him. But how could it have occurred? No one had missed him. He could not have been struck by a ball without his comrades noticing it. There was, consequently, a mystery, perhaps, of great importance. It was, therefore, necessary that the Emperor should be informed, for it was his wish that every occurence out of the ordinary line should be brought to his notice. The chieftain of the Guards himsef undertook to inform him.

The officer, having announced that he had matters of importance to communicate, was immediately admitted to the monarch's presence. Although the sovereign was worn out with fatigue, and it was now nearly daybreak, he had not retired, but the chieftain found him closeted with Morosini, engaged in earnest conversation. The officer, entering, knelt before his sovereign, who bade him speak.

"Your Majesty," said the officer, "what I have to say to you grieves me sorely: one of my best soldiers cannot be found."

The Emperor, who knew all his guards by name, enquired with deep interest:

"Who is it?"

"Your Majesty, it is Dimitrios Phocas."

Morosini, forgetting the imperial presence, sprang up, as though an electric shock had passed through him.

"Impossible!" he exclaimed; "Good Heavens! it cannot be!"

"Dimitrios Phocas?" repeated the Emperor; "are you not mistaken?"

"No, Sire, Dimitrios was the only one who failed to answer the call."

"Did he leave the city with the troops?"

"He did, Sire, most assuredly; he was present before we left our quarters, and I even exchanged words with him outside the walls, shortly before the first shot was fired from the Turkish camp."

"Did you see him since?"

"No, Sire, I did not."

"This is a mystery. He could not possibly have been struck by a ball, or it would have been noticed. There must be treachery."

"Not in Dimitrios?" exclaimed Morosini.

"No, Vincent, I did not mean that; but I am almost

afraid that we are surrounded by traitors; who can tell where the serpent, Nicolaus Lecapenos, is?"

Morosini stood dumbfounded.

The Emperor continued:

"No pains must be spared; let every quarter of the city be searched; send men outside of the walls, as much as prudence will permit, at least, as far as we proceeded last night; the Turks will not venture so near the city. I will grant myself no rest until Dimitrios is found."

"Your Majesty," said Morosini, may I depart? I have a painful yet cherished duty to perform. Dimitrios has entrusted to me the care of his sister."

"Yes, Vincent, go, and may the Mother of God protect you!"

The Venetian prostrated himself before his Majesty and retired. The Emperor, addressing the chieftain of the Guards, spoke:

"Are you perfectly sure that there is no traitor among your men?"

"I am, your Majesty; I trust each individual among them as much as I trust myself. You know that they are a select body of men, although foreigners, and that each one has been admitted only upon the highest recommendations."

"I cannot, then, possibly solve the mystery; truly, matters are darkening around us. Go now, do your duty; spare no pains; find Dimitrios for me. I will be ever grateful to you."

The officer arose and retired.

Reader, it is now morning; the bright sun shines over Constantinople; the bombardment was resumed at dawn. Return with me to the house of Dimitrios. Helena had not closed her eyes; she would have refused sleep had it presented itself. A great part of the night she had spent in prayer. The firing during the night had greatly alarmed her, and she trembled for the safety of her brother. Finally, the morning dawned, and she gladly welcomed its approach, for it would relieve her anxiety and bring her news of her brother. She had gone out into the court-yard, and she was sitting beside the fountain when Morosini was announced. Her heart beat rapidly; every nerve in her body trembled. What could this early visit indicate? Had anything happened to Dimitrios? She gave orders to the servant to admit the visitor, and Morosini entered. He was pale, though a forced smile played upon his lips. Helena saw at a glance that something unwonted had occurred; she sprang up quickly and extended her hands imploringly, as she exclaimed:

"Tell me, oh! tell me, where is my brother?"

"Be calm, my lady," said Morosini. "Do not be uselessly agitated."

"Oh, yes, yes." she cried out, "something has happened; tell me; leave me not in suspense; where is he?"

Morosini, fearing lest her anxiety should cause her more harm than the knowledge of the truth, gently broke the news to her.

The girl's face grew white; her head swam; there was a ringing in her ears; she threw up her hands, and, with a piercing shriek, she fell. Helena had fainted.

Morosini, alarmed, hastily summoned the servants. Two old trusty domestics, who had been with the family for years, ran forward, followed by Zoe, the old nurse, who loved her young mistress more than she loved herself. They bathed her forehead, applied various remedies, and carried her to her apartment. Morosini remained in the house until he was assured by the physician, who had been summoned, that there was no immediate danger. The latter, however, recommended absolute rest. When, after a long period of unconsciousness, the girl opened her eyes, there was a vacant stare in them. She seemed to recognize no one, and, from time to time, muttered the name of Dimitrios.

The day passed, but there was no news of the young Greek. The Emperor's orders had been strictly executed; no stone had been left unturned, but no clue to the mystery could be discovered. Dimitrios had disappeared, as if the earth had opened and swallowed him. The ruler of the Byzantine Empire was disconsolate, for, although the young man was far beneath him, he knew that one of his ancestors had been seated on the same throne he occupied, and, moreover, he was deeply attached to Dimitrios.

Morosini's grief knew no bounds. He offered great rewards for any clue that would lead to the discovery of his friend, but it was all of no avail. The mystery could not be unraveled.

Irene had been treacherously taken away from Constantinople, and now, Dimitrios had vanished. Dark forebodings filled the soul of Vincent Morosini.

CHAPTER XIII.

While a part of Constantinople was disturbed and lost in painful reflections on account of the sudden disappearance of Dimitrios, strange things were taking place within the Turkish camp. In a small tent, not far from the pavilion of the Sultan, sat upon the ground a man, apparently in the prime of life. His face was ferocious, resembling that of a blood-thirsty animal, yet there was a mildness in his eye and a peculiar kindly expression about his lips which contrasted strongly with the rest of his features. He held in his hands a manuscript book, with illuminated letters, which he was reading attentively. It was not written in the Turkish language, neither was it Greek, but the characters were unmistakably Latin or Roman. On close observation, you would not have failed to recognize the reader; it was no other than Selim whom we met at the gate of Adrianople.

It was the morning after the attempted sortie in which Dimitrios had disappeared. The dew drops hung pearl-like from the leaves, while a refreshing coolness filled the air; even the grass in the tent of Selim was damp, and he had spread upon it the thick rug upon which he was seated. Suddenly he was startled by the sound of footsteps outside of the tent. Hastily closing the book he was reading, he concealed it within the loose jacket that he wore, and looked angrily toward the entrance. A portion of the canvass that closed it was raised and a Turkish soldier entered. Giving Selim a military salute, he spoke:

"The Sultan desires your presence. This is the password," and he whispered into the ear of Selim, who, without a word of reply, arose, and, leaving the tent, directed his steps towards the Sultan's pavilion. It was surrounded by a detachment of soldiers. As he approached the entrance, an officer advanced to meet him and whispered:

"The password!"

In an equally low tone of voice, Selim replied:

"The triumph of the Koran!"

He was allowed to pass on. The pavilion of Mahomet II. was a wooden house, raised high above the ground, half Byzantine, half Moorish in style, and containing several apartments. A flight of stairs led up to the arched doorway. As Selim approached the door, he spoke to the attendant:

"I am Selim, the Sultan awaits me."

The guard replied:

"In the name of Allah, advance and follow me."

The soldier proceeding, Selim followed and he was admitted into the presence of the Turkish ruler, before whom he prostrated himself.

"Arise, Selim," spoke the Monarch, "may'st thou conquer thy enemies and may thy face be ever white!"

"May Allah protect thee, son of the Prophet!" replied Selim.

"Selim," said the Sultan, "we have been fortunate, Allah has this night not only delivered us from the snares intended for us by our enemies, but he has delivered one of the Christian dogs into our hands."

There was a peculiar smile upon the lips of Selim.

"Last night," continued the Sultan, "after the Greeks had retreated, and we were once more lulled to rest and calm repose in the full security of our strength, an incident occurred that might have proved injurious to us. One of the guards at the great battery, thinking he heard a rustling of leaves and an unwonted sound on the side of the hill on which the large cannon is mounted, directed his steps towards the spot whence the sound came. A good genius conducted him, for he had scarcely approached the cannon, when the figure of a man was seen to glide away. He immediately fired a shot, with one of his small arms, thus giving the alarm, the place was scoured, and, to our great and good fortune, a young Greek was captured. He was at once brought into my presence. I assure you, Selim, that I have seldom seen such a handsome countenance; and what a noble bearing! I said to myself: he would be an acquisition for the Prophet. What, think you, had brought him hither? A huge spike and a large hammer were found upon him. These sufficiently indicate his intentions. At all events, the stars have favored us, our cannon has been saved and we have been spared much annoyance. What think you, we should do with the young man?"

Selim looked like a tiger, his eyes flashed fire, his brows were knitted:

"Son of Allah," he exclaimed, "death is too good for him, he must be tortured."

"I will be merciful," replied the Sultan, "I have thought much over the matter, and have come to the following decision: if the Greek consents to embrace the religion of the Koran, he shall live; if not, he must die."

"Yes, and a horrible death," replied Selim.

The Sultan gazed at him in surprise. It was the first time that he had ever pleaded for the death of a captive.

"Selim," he spoke, "I knew that yours was not the heart of a woman, but I never knew that you delighted in the shedding of blood."

"I delight in justice," the other replied, then continued:

"Can I serve Mahomet in this matter?"

"You can, Selim. I entrust the prisoner to you. Be kind to him at first, endeavor to win him for the Prophet, leave nothing untried, promise him everything. Have patience, I grant him to you as your slave. If you succeed, he shall be free, but a greater reward shall be yours. If you fail, do with him as you list, torture him, let him suffer, and end his agony by death when he can live no longer."

The Sultan, placing a board and paper on his knee, wrote. Handing the document to Selim, he said:

"Here is my firman, show it to the officer of the guard, and he will have you conducted to the tent where the prisoner is in custody. You may go now."

Selim prostrated himself before the Sultan and departed. The signature of the Monarch worked like a talisman. Two soldiers were immediately detailed to conduct Selim to the prisoner. As he entered the tent, his eye fell upon a young man, half nude, who lay chained to a huge block of wood. Selim approached him, he raised up the head of the prisoner, it was Dimitrios Phocas. A look of intense surprise showed itself upon the face of the Turk. Turning towards the guards, he said:

"Unlock the prisoner's chains, and conduct him to my tent."

Within a quarter of an hour, Selim and the young Greek were alone in the tent of the former. The Turk was seated, while the Greek stood before him.

"Christian," said Selim in Greek, with a kindly voice, "what brought thee hither?".

"My duty to my country."

"Didst thou not know that thy life was in danger?"

"I was willing to sacrifice my life."

"Had'st thou forgotten Helena?"

Dimitrios was dumbfounded, he stared in mute surprise.

"Be not astonished, Dimitrios, I know you;" then, continuing in a low tone, Selim added:

"I will communicate to you a great secret, but promise me first that it shall never cross your lips, until you have my permission."

"I promise, if it is compatible with my conscience."

"Then listen. Dimitrios, you know me, you have seen me ere this."

The astonished look upon the face of Dimitrios grew more intense. Selim's voice changed completely, as he continued:

"Do you not remember the monk Gregorios?"

"Father Gregorios?" replied Dimitrios in astonishment, "do you know Father Gregorios? you have his voice now, but you had it not at first."

"I am Father Gregorios, my son. Sit beside me, Dimitrios, and you shall hear all. You recollect that I first met you at the outer porch of St. Sophia, on the western side, as we were both leaving the church. I accosted you, for there was something in your features that pleased me. I gained your confidence, you related to me matters concerning yourself and your family, my interest in you was awakened. You believed me to be a Greek monk, as my habit seemed to indicate; you were mistaken. I had not lied to you, no! I was indeed from the monastery of Agios Kyriani, for I had spent there two months quite recently. I was also a monk, but not in the sense in which you understood it. Now, Dimitrios, relying on your fidelity, I will tell you all. I am a Latin Christian, my name is Gregorio de Los Santos, and my country, the Kingdom of Aragon, for I was born at Lerida in the principality of Catalonia. I am not only a Latin, but I am a religious and priest of the Latin Church, in communion with the See of Rome. You look surprised, but, astonishing though it be, it is true. Were this known, my head would fall. Thus, Dimitrios, my life is in your hands, but, perhaps, your happiness is in mine."

"Fear nothing, Father Gregorios, the ties of a common Christianity unite us. Please, continue."

"I belong to the Order of La Merced for the Redemption of Captives, an order which was established at Barcelona, in 1218, by Peter Nolasco, Raymond of Pennafort, and King James I. of Aragon. Our object is the deliverance of captives who are in the power of the infidel. We even take a vow by which we bind ourselves to surrender our liberty and remain as slaves instead of our brethren. It was my fortune to be called upon by Divine Providence to fulfill my promise. More than twenty years have elapsed since I have seen any of my brethren, seldom in that time has it been my privilege to offer up the Holy Sacrifice, but a loving Providence has sustained me in the midst of many difficulties. Truly, I have become anathema for my brethren. I will relate to you how it all occurred. I was a young man, full of fervor, and I had lately been ordained priest in our monastery of Our Lady of Puch. We had heard of the capture of Thessalonica, and learned that a number of Christian captives, both Geeks and Latins, had been carried off to Aleppo. Our superiors determined to send two religious thither with large sums of money for a ransom. Their choice fell upon me. With one of my brethren, I sailed from Barcelona, in 1432, through the Mediterranean as far as Smyrna, whence we journeyed by land to Aleppo. We had large sums of money contributed by charitable persons in Christendom, and we were enabled to ransom a number of captives. There was a poor Greek woman, advanced in years, who had fallen into the hands of an inhuman Turk. Her lot was pitiful. Subjected day after day to the most cruel treatment, and made to perform labors far above her strength, the poor creature seemed about to succumb. How gladly would I have paid her ransom! But my money had all been spent. I remembered my vow, and offered myself to her Turkish master to be his slave in her stead. The Turk seeing in me an able-bodied young man, considered the exchange favorable, and let the old woman depart. She went away heaping blessings upon my head. My companion took her in charge and returned to Europe with his captives; I remained in bondage. I had expected to be subjected to the same cruel treatment, but the contrary was the case. For some reason or other my master took a liking to me. I was most faithful in the performance of my duty, I was skilled in medicine and thus rendered many a service, and, moreover, I amused him with certain arts in which I was proficient. For instance I constructed a piece of mechanism, an automaton, that would walk towards him as the door of his apartment opened. Moreover, I played the harp with a master-touch. This man being an officer of high grade in the army, I followed him to the wars, and I was thus brought into relations with the Sultan. My knowledge and tact gained me universal esteem. The impression I made upon Sultan Amurath II. was such, that he obtained my freedom and attached me to the army. With his successor, Mahomet, I have enjoyed the same favor. I have rendered immense services by my medical skill, and the boldness of my manner has made me respected by the soldiers.

"Some persons possess the power of contorting their features and taking the expression of any emotion. I am one of these. Though never gifted by nature with any degree of beauty, I have rendered my countenance still more ugly by the habitual savage expression I have assumed in order the better to awe my inferiors, who, if they knew me, would be my enemies. My position has been a difficult one, indeed. Brought into constant relations with the Mahometan religion, I have had an incessant struggle to avoid practising it, but circumstances have favored me. I speak with respect of the prophet, as I would of some great ancestor of the Turks. In fact, I have become a Turk, in all but their religion. Several times I have had the opportunity to escape, but I have never availed myself of it, knowing the immense spiritual succor I am enabled to render the Christian captives who fall into the hands of the Mussulmans. Many a one I have saved from death, and to hundreds have I brought the consolations of our holy Religion in their last moments. When you met me in Constantinople, disguised as a Greek monk, I had gone thither to receive myself those consolations from which

I am so frequently deprived. I have kept myself informed of matters happening in your city, by means of a shrewd countryman of mine, whom you shall meet. Fortuny is his name. Thus, Dimitrios, you know my history."

The youth, who had listened with the greatest attention, now spoke:

"Father, I can scarcely believe my ears. Your narrative is wonderful. How good Divine Providence is!"

"Dimitrios, you are safe in my hands. I will restore you to Helena, but not now. Have patience. However, to relieve your anxiety, I will find means to communicate with her this very night, and the day after to-morrow, you shall hear from your sister. Write a letter to her immediately, and send it to me."

"How can I ever thank you, Father Gregorio?" exclaimed the grateful youth.

"Fear nothing, my son, answered the priest, Divine Providence watches over you. I will provide for you a tent, and, to avoid suspicion, place a guard before it. Bear with this small inconvenience for the sake of Helena. Farewell now."

Gregorio arose and conducted Dimitrios to the door, placing him in the hands of a guard, to whom, in the Turkish language, he gave orders to keep a strict watch over the prisoner, but to treat him with respect. Gregorio, or Selim, as we shall still call him, re-entered his tent.

Within a half hour a guard entered bearing a letter from Dimitrios to Helena. Selim placed it in his bosom and nodded to the guard to retire; he then took out the book we had seen in his hands in the morning, and continued to read. It was his breviary.

When Dimitrios found himself alone, an inexpressible feeling of sadness came over him. He was far from those he knew and loved, and he could imagine their state of anxiety on his account. Moreover, although he had found a friend, still he was a prisoner, and deprived of his liberty, and, besides, in the midst of enemies. His deed had been a rash one, but it was actuated by the purest motives of patriotism. It was with mingled feelings of awe and self-satisfaction that he revolved its circumstances in his mind, though he, at the same time, feared the blame of the Emperor and of his friends. The thought, also, of the amount of suffering he must have cost Helena, plunged him into the deepest grief; but, alas! it was a thought that came too late. What had brought Dimitrios to this sad plight? On leaving Constantinople, the night before, he had set his heart upon being one of the first to mount the Turkish battery, and he had even provided himself with tools for spiking the cannon. When the order to retreat was given, his heart sank within him; he saw how a glorious opportunity was about to escape him. Dimitrios was a creature of impulse, and he had many a hard lesson yet to learn before he would overcome the impetuosity of his temperament. Without reflecting on the dangers to which he was exposing himself, without even a second thought, he blindly decided to attempt alone what several companies of soldiers had not ventured to undertake. Profiting by the darkness to evade observation, he glided out of the ranks, and literally groped his way to the Turkish battery. He might have succeeded, had not the sharp ear of the Turkish guard detected a faint sound made by the rustling of some bushes, against which he brushed. The reader knows the rest. Now that he found himself alone, and calm reflection had taken the place of the excitement of the previous night, Dimitrios saw into his rashness, but it was too late. The thought of Helena, and her anxiety, tormented him, and he would have given the world for wings to fly into Constantinople, and be with his sister. The only comfort he found was in the promise of Father Gregorio to communicate with her that very night.

Selim discovered, on mature reflection, that it would not be such an easy task to fulfil his promise, but he was a man of unbounded resources when there was a question of forming plans, and one who never gave up. If he had undertaken a thing, he went through fire and water to accomplish it. For a long time, after reciting his office, he sat in a pensive mood, revolving in his mind various means of reaching Helena through a letter, but difficulties seemed to increase around him. The camp was well guarded, and it appeared almost impossible to leave it without exposing himself to great risk, nor was there a single person within his reach on whom he might rely. Finally, his eye brightened, a smile lit up his countenance. He arose, left his tent, and walked directly toward that of the prisoner. Pushing aside the canvas, he entered.

"Dimitrios," said he, "can you give me any information concerning Nicolaus Lecapenos?"

"I can," was the answer, and Dimitrios related briefly all that had occurred. Gregorio looked sad when he heard of the murder of Leila, and exclaimed, in a mournful voice:

"Poor girl! God is just. Thank you, Dimitrios," he added, "I shall soon find means to send a letter to Helena, meanwhile, be of good courage."

Selim left the tent, and, for a time, paced up and down as though greatly preoccupied; finally, he moved towards the Sultan's pavilion. An officer of the Janizaries advanced to meet him.

"I cannot give you the password now," said Selim, "but, think you that there is a possibility of seeing the Sultan?"

"It is exceedingly doubtful," answered the officer, "but I will see; tarry here awhile."

Within a brief period he returned, saying:

"You may enter."

Selim, after the preliminary ceremonies, thus addressed the monarch:

"Sublime Lord, I have learned that Nicolaus has been condemned to death; however, he has escaped from prison; but he is in imminent danger. He may be useful to us; should we not endeavor to save him? He is a bold, daring and shrewd man, and such men are not found every day."

"True," replied the Sultan, "but how can we communicate with him?"

"I have hit upon a plan. If Nicolaus is found, he will surely be put to death, for it is known that he has betrayed the Greeks. On the other hand, in his present position, he can be of no service to us. You may be assured that the Emperor Constantine will do anything to gain your favor. Now, my plan is this: The young Greek you have captured, will be of little use. He has never borne arms until now; he could not possibly stand any hardships, and he lacks prudence. Offer to exchange him for Nicolaus."

"Would the Greeks be willing to make the exchange?"

"They will do anything to conciliate Sultan Mahomet."

"But is it not better to have Nicolaus in Constantinople?"

"Since he has been once caught, no disguise would be safe. His usefulness in the city is at an end."

"How will you communicate with the Greeks? I am absolutely unwilling to treat with them; they shall not for a moment imagine that I desire any favor."

"I will send a letter into Constantinople this very night by means of an arrow, if I may have the permission of your Highness. That letter will seem to come from a private source. The Greeks will make use of it, and, if they find Nicolaus, they will certainly offer him to you, and be glad to be rid of him. All I need is your permission to cross the lines to-night."

"It is granted. But are you willing to give up your slave thus easily?"

"For the common good, I am; and, after the city falls, there will be no lack of slaves."

The Sultan wrote, and, handing the paper to Selim, said:

"Go, and do as you have spoken."

In a half hour from then, Selim had passed the lines, and he was on his way to the city. A bow was strung from his shoulder, while several arrows were protruding from a quiver. To two of these a letter was attached.

A black pall of darkness covered the earth; not an object could be distinguished, but Selim knew the environs of Constantinople perfectly. He was now only a few yards from the ditch. Noiselessly and by stealth he had approached. Fixing one of the arrows to his bow, he raised it, and, in a moment, the improvised letter-carrier went whizzing through the air. Selim had measured his distance and the strength of his bow, and he knew exactly how far it would reach. A few seconds later, the other arrow followed; the priest had accomplished his mission.

CHAPTER XIV.

With great anxiety, Dimitrios had waited for the end of the long monotonous day which had been unusually warm, and which, he hoped, would bring him an answer to his letter. Not a ripple had stirred the surface of the Bosphorus, and the vessels upon it had lain completely motionless, while their white sails flapped hither and thither, or hung lifeless against the masts. No breath of air had fanned the heated brow of the sentinels around the camp or the gunners on the various batteries. Forming a strong contrast with the universal stillness of nature, was the din of strife that filled the air. The Turkish cannon had poured forth deadly fire all day, which was feebly answered by the guns of Constantinople, but, instead, the dreaded Greek fire had not been idle, and wherever the besieged had found an opportunity of reaching the Turkish ships, they had loaded their pistons and sent the fiery dragons whizzing through the air to burn more than one Turkish vessel and inflict unutterable torture on the soldiers and sailors of the enemy who were unfortunate enough to fall victims to it.

Towards evening, the fire of the cannon had gradually ceased, and the combatants on both sides were preparing to rest from the deadly labors of the day. More than one Turkish corpse had been dragged away from the scene of battle by comrades swearing dire vengeance upon the Greeks.

Finally the long wished-for night arrived, to give rest to man and beast. Gradually its shades had fallen upon the landscape, and the towers of Constantinople were scarcely visible in the gloom. As the darkness of night had taken the place of the sweltering heat of the day, and a refreshing breeze was wafted from the Bosphorus towards the land, Selim went forth from the Turkish camp, protected by an order of the Sultan. Alone and silent he pursued his way toward the city, lost in the gloom of night. The Turkish soldiers must have wondered what carried him abroad at that hour, but none dared interrogate him, for Selim was feared by all, and they knew that he enjoyed the confidence of the Sultan.

Approaching near to the ditch, until he could almost throw a stone into the city, he placed his fingers to his lips and gave a shrill and prolonged whistle. It was quickly answered from the ramparts, above which appeared a light in the glare of which the figure of a man was seen, armed with a bow and directing an arrow towards Selim, who, striking a light, held a lantern high above his head. The arrow was sent whizzing through the air and it fell at the distance of a yard to the right of Selim, who had followed it with his eyes as much as the darkness permitted. He had heard it fall, and directed by his light, he walked toward it. The arrow lay upon the ground, and another whistle from Selim announced that the message had reached its destination. The lights were extinguished and all was dark and silent as before.

When Selim reached the Turkish camp, he proceeded directly to his tent. Striking a light, he examined the arrow and found two small letters attached to it. One was directed to Selim, the other to Dimitrios. In the former he read:

"All efforts will be made to find Nicolaus, and, if they prove successful, a flag of truce will be sent at once with an offer of exchange. Farewell."

Taking the letter for Dimitrios in his hand, Selim at once proceeded to the tent of the prisoner. As he entered, the Greek arose, and, with an anxious expression upon his countenance, advanced to meet his benefactor.

"Be of good cheer, my boy," said Selim, "I have an answer to your letter. I knew it would arrive in due season."

Dimitrios grasped the paper with trembling hand and palpitating heart. Opening it, he read as follows:

"Dearest Brother! It is impossible to describe the feelings of gladness that took possession of my soul, when I learned that you were alive. I have been ill, very ill, but, thank God! this most acceptable news has greatly revived me. Still I shudder when I think that you are among the Turks, although it is with the deepest feelings of gratitude towards God, that I learn that even there you have found a friend and protector. Heaven grant that Nicolaus may be discovered, and that I may soon embrace my brother again! I cease not to pray for you, and to invoke the intercession of Holy Mary that you may return to me. Our friend, Morosini, does all in his power to console me. The Emperor is, also, very concerned about your safety, and he will spare no sacrifice to obtain your release. Have confidence, brother, and place your trust in God, we shall soon meet again.   Your sister,   HELENA."

The countenance of Dimitrios brightened, as his eyes ran quickly over the lines. Handing the letter to Selim, he said:

"Read, Father. Thank God, she feels consoled."

Selim took the letter and read it.

"God is good, my dear son," he said, "I feel that all

will be well yet. Tomorrow I will see you again, rest well, may the Holy Angels guard you!"

With these words he left the tent of Dimitrios and retired to his own. He found a soldier awaiting him.

"Selim," said the military, "tomorrow the army is to move onward, we are to approach nearer to the city. Constantinople is doomed. It may take a long time, for there is much vitality still left in the old ruin, but it is surely ours. I am rejoiced that we are to approach nearer, for this everlasting pounding away at the old walls is beginning to be tedious; it is like wasting powder. Moreover, I am anxious for a little sport."

"You may have more than you expect," replied Selim, "and, besides, you may be badly scorched before you reach the city, if you ever succeed in going so far. Don't forget the Greek fire."

"It is the only thing I am afraid of," answered the soldier, "but tell me, Selim, (you seem to know all), where did they ever get that infernal thing from?"

"The Greek fire was invented about the year 667, by a certain Callinicus, of Heliopolis, and brought by him to Constantinople."

"The fiends devour him! what is the accursed stuff made of?"

"It is a composition of naphtha, pitch and sulphur."

"By Mahomet! They say that nothing resists it."

"You are right. Water does not extinguish it, and it holds on to wood tenaciously. If it ever takes hold of you, I assure you, that you will long to be in paradise with Mahomet!"

"Confound those Greeks! If I ever penetrate into Constantinople, I will give them as much Turkish fire as they can digest, and let them tell me then which is worse, Turkish or Greek fire. But I was going to forget what I had come for. Hassan has arrived at the camp, and he was asking for you. He was as hungry as a wolf, and he devoured nearly a whole ox."

"Is Hassan here? Bring him to me at once."

Selim entered his tent, and the soldier departed. Within a brief period, the curtain at the entrance was raised, and a Turk of fierce visage, with an immense sword at his side, stood before Selim.

"Fortuny," exclaimed the latter in pure Castilian, "*Que barbaridad!* how unexpected this is!"

"I am exceedingly glad to see you, Father," answered Fortuny in the Catalan dialect, and, continuing in Castilian, he added: "but let us converse in a low tone, *porque las paredes oyen*, the walls have ears."

"Let us be seated," answered Selim in a subdued voice, taking the hint, "and relate to me what you have heard and seen."

Both men sat down on a carpet, in Turkish fashion, crossing their legs.

"Father Gregorio," began Fortuny, "Alas! I have no agreeable news to communicate to you. Nicolaus brought himself into serious difficulty by a most atrocious deed."

"I have heard it, Fortuny. Poor unfortunate Leila! I know it all."

"You know of the death of Leila? How could you have heard it?"

"Forego that question for the present, you shall hear later, but tell me now where you have been, and how you came hither."

Fortuny related his last interview with Nicolaus, and continued:

"I was determined to go to Thessalonica, even if Nicolaus had not requested me to do so, but I left him under the impression that I was undertaking the journey for the sake of the gold he had promised. I left Constantinople shortly before the siege began, on an Aragoneze vessel, which, with an excellent wind, soon landed me at Thessalonica. My first thought was to seek for the family of Diogenes, and I consequently directed my steps towards the Church of the Holy Apostles. I looked for the house and found it without difficulty. But, imagine my cruel disappointment, when I discovered that it was uninhabited and without the slightest sign of life. I enquired from every possible source, but no one could give me the slightest clue to the whereabouts of Diogenes and his children. All I could learn was that strangers had been there, but, that, a few days since, they had left the place in company of the Turkish escort that had brought them. No one could tell whither they had gone. My search had been vain. As quickly as I could, I returned to the shores of the Bosphorus."

"Poor Dimitrios!" exclaimed Selim. "Fortuny, say nothing to him concerning your voyage to Thessalonica."

"It is useless to caution me, for I will have no opportunity of seeing Dimitrios."

"You are mistaken, my friend, Dimitrios is here. It is from him that I learned of the sad fate of the woman Leila."

"Dimitrios here? How can that be?"

Selim related what had occured, and continued:

"Fortuny, my faithful friend, we must find Diogenes; you will help me, will you not?"

"If I should have to sail to the land of the Antipodes, if any such monsters exist, I will find them. That is, if they are in the land of the living."

"Well said, my trusty Fortuny; I know you will succeed, for you have yet to fail."

"Do not flatter too much, Father Gregorio, I do what I can. But let us now speak of more agreeable matters. I know that you are very abstemious, but I have an elastic stomach. I have concealed under my jacket a flask of delightful Spanish wine. Ah! when I look at the sparkling liquid, I seem to sit in the shadow of La Virgen del Pilar, at Zaragoza, where I lived for many years; I am home again in Barcelona, on the blue waters of the Mediterranean, when I quaff the delightful fluid."

"For heaven's sake, Fortuny, what are you doing? If a Turk should happen to come in at this moment and find you drinking wine, we would be ruined. It would be as bad as to find you eating pork."

"No fear! Father, they will never find me eating pork, whenever I have anything else; but, as for wine, they quaff it themselves occasionally on the sly, when they think the Prophet in paradise is looking in another direction and he has not his eyes upon them."

"That makes no difference. As a rule the Turks observe this law of the Koran with scrupulous exactitude and you will surely draw upon yourself their enmity if they find you transgressing it."

"But it only takes a second, Father Gregorio," and before the priest could interpose, Fortuny had brought the bottle to his lips and taken a strong draught.

Hastily concealing the flask, he said:

"Now, Father, I am ready to go to the end of the world, yea, to fight Mahomet himself if he were to come on earth. But, you know, I must have my wine, as much as the German must have his beer."

"You said you wanted to speak of something agreeable; what had you to say?"

"O! yes. I had mentioned the word Antipodes, do you believe in the existence of those beings?"

"A strange question, Fortuny."

"You know, Father, I delight in those questions. I have sailed down the African coast on one of the ships sent out by Prince Henry, the Navigator, and it is natural that my mind should occasionally revert to a topic, which, at present, occupies much attention."

"Well," replied Selim, "there are differences of opinion, some believing in the existence of Antipodes, while others maintain that this opinion is heretical. Listen to the words of the famous Cardinal d'Ailly, Bishop of Cambrai, who died some years since, in 1420. In his *Imago Mundi—Image of the World*, he writes:

"'The earth is spherical, and the western ocean relatively small. Aristotle maintains against Ptolomy, that more than a fourth of the earth is inhabited, and Averrhoes holds the same opinion. The Stagyrite affirms also that the sea is small between the western coasts of Spain and the eastern shores of India. There is here a question not of Spain proper, but of Spain extended, or Africa. Seneca assures us that this sea can be crossed in a few days with a favorable wind.'"

"The Cardinal thus believes that the earth is round, that the eastern shores of India are west of Spain, and, the consequence is, that he believes that the other side of the earth is inhabited, and that, therefore, Antipodes exist."

"Who, did you say, was the author of the work you cited?"

"Cardinal Pierre d'Ailly, or, as they call him in Latin, Petrus de Alliaco."

"Father Gregorio, I have heard of that author ere this. It is very strange that you should recall his name. I had almost forgotten a conversation held some six months ago, which made a deep impression upon me. You remember that I once arrived very suddenly in Adrianople, as suddenly as I came hither to-day? Well, I had just come from the Ægean sea, on a Genoese vessel bound for Pera. I boarded her at Crete, and we stopped for some time at Tinos to take on a cargo of figs and grapes, besides a lot of silk that the vessel was to take back to Italy. There was a young lad on board with whom I became very imtimate, and we had many an interesting conversation. I found him a most intelligent youth and he said that he had studied at the University of Pavia. One evening, just after leaving Tinos, we were leaning against the bulwarks, engaged in discussing cosmography. Cristoforo, for thus was the boy known to all his shipmates, Cristoforo, suddenly pointing towards the west, exclaimed: 'I have a presentiment that my name has a deep significance. Yes, I feel that the day will come when I shall carry Christ to the inhabitants of unknown regions beyond the Dark Ocean.' Father Gregorio, never in my life have I seen a face that bore so much the marks of inspiration as the countenance of young Christoforo Colombo did at that moment. Turning to me, and taking in his hand a book he had been holding under his arms, he said: 'Here, Fortuny, here is a wonderful book. It was written by Cardinal Petrus de Alliaco. I simply devour it. It contains wonderful things.'*

---

*There exists in the Columbian Library, at Seville, a copy of the *Imago Mundi*, printed between 1480 and 1483, thus a few years before the discovery of America. The margins are filled with notes by the hand of Columbus himself. It is by no means improbable that he was already acquainted with this author in the early years of his life.

Your citing the words of this author has recalled this conversation to my mind. Young Colombo was a firm believer in the existence of Antipodes. We parted from each other at Pera, and I have never heard of him since."

"Well, Fortuny," said Selim, "I too believe that the Antipodes are no fable, and I am not the only one. When I was in Barcelona, I met a young Dominican friar from the house of his order in Salamanca, the convent of San Esteban, and he assured me that it was an opinion shared by several of his Fathers. However, Fortuny, we have had enough of this learned, or, as you are pleased to call it, agreeable cenversation for the present. You must be tired, I surely am, for it is late. You may share my tent."

Fortuny thanked his host, and, in a short time, both friends were lost in sleep.

CHAPTER XV.

Long ere the day dawned, the Turkish army had moved nearer to the city, so that when the first rays of the sun broke upon it, the astonished eyes of the Greeks beheld the change that had taken place noiselessly, and as if by magic. Even the Sultan's pavilion had been removed without difficulty, as it rested upon a system of rollers. The besieged had scarcely time to recover from their surprise, when the fourteen Turkish batteries opened fire upon them. In the camp the noise was deafening; the very earth trembled. The Greeks endeavored to reply, but their fire was feeble, for no sooner had they mounted their cannon in one spot, than the old walls shook to such an extent that they were obliged to desist. However, whenever a detachment of Turks happened to approach near enough, they would sling their dreaded Greek fire at them, thus sending many a Turk to the other world. They also succeeded in setting fire to more than one of the mediæval war-engines which the Turks had been endeavoring to place into position. The distant report of cannon showed also that things were lively on the water, especially at the entrance to the Golden Horn, which was defended by the Greek ships.

Dimitrios heard the reports of cannon, and he chafed with impatience at the thought that he was powerless to aid his country. He could not leave his tent before the arrival of Selim, and, though the sun was already high in the heavens, the latter had not yet visited him. Dimitrios grew uneasy. Had something occurred? Of course, he knew that the army had approached nearer to Constantinople, for his own tent had been moved, together with the rest, and he had been obliged to assist. The thought of making his escape had presented itself to his mind, but the evident uselessness of the attempt, and, above all, the fear that he should injure Selim, deterred him. While many painful thoughts were passing through his mind, the door of his tent suddenly opened and a guard entered, saying:

"I have orders to conduct you to the tent of Selim."

Dimitrios accompanied the soldier, and, in a few moments, he stood before his friend, who thus addressed him:

"Dimitrios, I have taxed your patience, but important matters demanded my attention; however, I sent for you as soon as possible."

"Father, is there any news from the city? I am growing anxious."

"Be not alarmed, my son; you know that such matters require time. Exercise patience now as a penance for your rashness. If, within a few days, Nicolaus is not discovered, I have other plans. Sit down and let us converse. We are comparatively safe here, for the cannon of the Greeks do little damage."

"Father Gregorious, I would converse with you on a very serious topic. Our life is so uncertain, it is well to be on the safe side. I have, thus far, never had a doubt of the righteousness of our cause—I mean that of the Greek Church. I have studied history carefully, and all seemed so clear. But, I cannot say why of late a strange feeling of inquietude has come over me, and the thought forces itself upon my mind: suppose, after all, that we are wrong, and that the Latins are right, as the Emperor and the Patriarch think. I mentioned this to an archimandrite of my acquaintance not long ago, and he told me not to trouble my mind about it, that such doubts would come. But this has not satisfied me. Whenever I am alone, my thoughts necessarily fall back upon this subject, even in spite of the inexpressible anguish I am enduring from anxiety for Irene, and fears for Helena. I know that you are a man of God; can you not relieve my mind?"

"My dear boy," replied the priest, "if you felt sure that the Greek Church is schismatic, and that in the Roman Church alone the true Church of Christ is to be found, would you hesitate to make a change?"

"Not one single instant," replied the young man, "even though it were necessary to sacrifice that which is dearest to me on earth: the love of Irene, and of my sister, Helena."

"You are a brave boy, but let us hope that such a sacrifice will not be required. Did you ever pray that the Holy Spirit might enlighten you?"

"It is my constant prayer."

"You shall have that light, my child; doubt it not. In this matter there is really only one thing to settle, only one vital question, and that is this: Is the Pope of Rome the Vicar of Christ; are all Christians bound to live in communion with him, and submit to his decrees? All else is secondary. If this question is proved, all has been proved."

"You know, Father, I have been taught to look upon the Pope as a usurper and a tyrant."

"I know it, my son, but it is not too late to be undeceived."

"Well, I am willing to be enlightened."

"Thus far, Dimitrios, you have studied only from one standpoint, that of the Greek Church; but, in this matter, we must go back to the time before the schism, when we were all one, when we all believed the same, when we were all subject to the Pope. We must see what all believed then, why they believed it, and why some changed their belief and broke with the Pope."

As Selim finished the last words, loud shouts and cries of joy were heard on the outside. He rushed to the door and enquired for the reason of the tumult.

"We have hit the mark," cried a veteran; "the tough old walls are beginning to yield."

"Is there a breach?" asked Selim.

"No, not yet, but large pieces are falling. See! there it goes," and, as he spoke, he pointed towards the city.

Selim gazed and saw that pieces of the wall between the Palace of the Hebdomon, in the suburb of Blachernae, and the gate of Polyandrion, were flying in splinters.

"This looks serious," he said.

Again he re-entered the tent, and, addressing Dimitrios, said:

"It was only a better shot than the ordinary ones. I thought that the whole wall was coming down. If you desire, I will proceed."

"You will oblige me greatly, Father, but will you first allow me to ask you a question?"

"Certainly, my son."

"Does the Latin Church recognize the validity of our orders?"

"Undoubtedly. The valid administration of the Sacrament of Holy Orders does not depend upon jurisdiction. If the one who ordains is truly a Bishop, and he has the intention of doing what the Church of Christ intends; if, at the same time, all other essential requisites are present, the candidate is validly ordained, even though the ordaining Bishop be a heretic or a schismatic. For that reason the Church did not require a second ordination in the case of those Greek Bishops and priests who returned to the communion of the See of Rome. For instance: there is Cardinal Joannes Bessarion. This learned man was born at Trebizond. He must be now about sixty years of age. Well, in 1423, Bessarion became a monk of St. Basil. In 1437, John Paleologos made him Bishop of Nicaea. He accompanied the Emperor to Italy, and he has remained there ever since, enjoying the favor of the Holy See, so much so, that Pope Eugene IV. conferred upon him the dignity of Cardinal. I am sure that Bessarion would become Pope, were he not a Greek."

"Thank you, Father; now proceed, for our time may be limited."

"If we ascend to the beginning of the schism, which was under Photius, in the middle of the ninth century, we find that, until then, the Greeks had acknowledged the supremacy of the Pope. But why? I will seek for the answer to this question among those whom you revere and love, the early Fathers of the Greek Church."

"Do the Greek Fathers teach the Supremacy of the Roman Pontiff?"

"They do, my son. Listen. You subscribe to the Council of Chalcedon. Well, this Council was presided over by the legates of Pope Leo. The Fathers of the Council call the Church of Rome the head of the churches, and, after the reading of a letter of Pope Leo, they all exclaimed: 'We all believe thus . . . Peter has thus spoken through Leo.' They also declare that Leo 'has been constituted interpreter of the voice of Blessed Peter to all men.' The Greek historian, Sozomen, tells us that the decision of the Church of the Romans in a matter of faith, was accepted by all the churches of the East. Ascending higher in antiquity, we hear the Council of Ephesus, in 431, assure us that it was guided by Pope Celestine, whom it calls Our 'Most Holy Father.'"

"From the Greek historian, Socrates, in the fifth century, we learn that the Pope was appealed to as judge, in the case of St. Athanasius. The same is told us by Theodoret, also a Greek Father. St. Cyril of Alexandria, calls the Pope the Archbishop of the whole Universe. Your great St. John Chrysostom, Patriarch of Constantinople, appealed to Pope Innocent against his persecutors. St. Gregory of Nazianzen, writes: 'The faith (of Rome) was of old, and still is now, right, binding the whole West by the saving word, as is just in her who presides over all, reverencing the whole harmonious teaching of God.'"

"The Greek Council of Sardica, in the year 347, teaches clearly that an appeal may be had to the Bishop of Rome against the decision of other Bishops."

"St. Irenæus, in the second century, speaks of the Church of Rome as the greatest of the churches; possessing a more powerful principality; with which it is necessary that every church agree; and in which Apostolic tradition has been preserved. I might thus continue, but let what I have said suffice."

"Father, you have given me great information. I was

never acquainted with these citations. You have opened before my eyes a new field of research; if ever I find leisure to devote myself to study, I will, most assuredly, explore it. But, tell me, what is your opinion of the beginning of the separation or schism?"

"If I may be outspoken, I must assure you that I think the cause lies primarily, and, as it were, in germ, in the jealousy which existed between the East and the West. From time immemorial, almost, there has been a tendency in Constantinople to place the Patriarch of that city on an equal footing with the Bishop of Rome. The final development arrived when Photius became Patriarch. This most learned man of his time was at first an intruder, and not the rightful Patriarch. The schism, begun under him, was, for a time, healed, but it was renewed again some years later, about 1053, when Michael Cerularius succeeded in withdrawing the eastern Bishops from communion with the West, on account of a discrepancy in doctrine, and a few minor differences in discipline. But, once more, this separation from the See of Rome was an innovation, and entirely opposed to the teaching of the early Fathers and the Councils."

"After all, then," said Dimitrios, "perhaps the Emperor is right. Father, I will continue to reflect most seriously upon this subject."

He had scarcely ended the sentence, when another wild shout arose, which reached from one end of the line to the other.

"Let us go out," said Selim.

Leaving the tent, they took up their position on a commanding eminence near by, whence they could overlook the entire scene. The balls from the large brass cannon were striking hard and fast upon the wall of which, now and anon, a huge piece would fall.

"Poor Greeks!" said Selim, "their end is nigh. Do you know what the present Pope, Nicolas V., wrote to them some time ago? These are his words: 'Long time have you abused the patience of God, by persisting in your schism. God is waiting, as in the parable, to see whether the fig-tree, which has been tended with such care, will, at last, yield its fruit; but, if within three years, it shall bear none, the tree will be hewn down, and the Greeks will be overwhelmed with the justice of God.' Do not these words seem sadly prophetic?"

Dimitrios could not help remembering the day when he first met Father Gregorios on the threshold of St. Sophia; his venerable aspect had brought to mind so forcibly the Prophet Jeremias, and now, as he heard those dreadful words uttered by his lips, they seemed to fall upon Constantinople as those of the Prophets of the Old Testament had fallen upon Jerusalem.

"My poor, unfortunate country!" lamented Dimitrios, "is there no salvation for thee? Father," he continued, "I love your society, but I long to re-enter Constantinople, but, alas! hope is dying out in my heart. Tell me, Father, would I injure you if I should effect my escape?"

"No, my son, you would not injure me, for I could show that you escaped without my co-operation. Besides, the Turks are not likely to trouble themselves concerning an individual prisoner, whom they are inclined to look upon as a fool; even had they a desire to injure me, they would abstain from doing so, for I am too useful to them."

"See!" exclaimed Selim, pointing towards the city, "what is that? Do you see that multitude of men? The Greeks are issuing forth from Constantinople."

Dimitrios looked in the direction indicated, and, verily, proceeding from the gate Polyandrion, over an improvised bridge, marched a small army in battle array. Spears and pikes glittered in the sunshine, which caused the armor of the soldiers to glisten like polished silver. Like one compact mass they advanced. Immediately the Turkish cannon were directed upon the multitude. The guns from Constantinople belched forth flashes of fire and clouds of smoke in reply, as if heedless of th danger to the walls. The Turkish balls flew over the heads of the Greeks as they advanced.

"Bravo! Bravo!" exclaimed Dimitrios, "oh, how I wish I were there!"

"Restrain your ardor, my young man," said Selim, calmly. " See! a Turkish regiment is forming in line of battle; there will be a hand-to-hand encounter. Look! the Sultan has come out of his pavilion. Beside him stands Mustapha Pacha, one of his trusty servants. The affair is serious, Dimitrios."

Meanwhile, the Greeks marched steadily onward, heedless of the Turkish fire. The Standard of the Emperor floated above the multitude; beside it, fluttering in the breeze, was that of Genoa.

"Come, Father, come," said Dimitrios, "can we not advance to the front? I will, at least, behold the scene in which I cannot act a part."

"I will go to the front," said Selim, "I am always where danger is greatest; my services may be required but I cannot take you with me. It would be considered treason."

"At least, let me stand where I can see the fight. May I not place myself near yonder tree?"

Dimitrios pointed to a tree at one of the outposts, beside which stood a horse, from which the rider had shortly before dismounted.

Selim beckoned to a Turk. The latter advanced; it was Fortuny.

"Hassan," said Selim, in a loud voice, and in the Turkish language, with a significant twinkle of his eye, "I confide to you this man; take him where he may behold the destruction of his countrymen, but remember, your life shall answer for him."

Selim pointed to the tree.

Fortuny, drawing his scimitar, took Dimitrios by the arm and led him to the place indicated.

"Where are you going with that Greek, Hassan?" queried a Turk, "are you about to cut off his head?"

"No, but he is going to see other heads cut off."

The Turk laughed. When Fortuny and Dimitrios were alone, the former whispered:

"Fear nothing, young man, I will not harm thee."

They reached the tree. Dimitrios gazed in the direction of the combatants, who were fast approaching each other. The eyes of all the spectators were turned in the same direction. Suddenly Dimitrios disengaged himself from the light grasp of Fortuny, and, with one bound, he sprang towards the horse. The seeming Turk, noticing this, wheeled around, and, raising his scimitar, as if about to strike, rushed upon Dimitrios, but, in his haste, he stumbled and fell heavily, as if by accident. Meanwhile, in less time than it takes to think of it, Dimitrios had loosed the animal and sprung into the saddle. Kicking it under its ribs, he darted off towards the city with the speed of lightning. Hearing the sound of horses' hoofs, the Turks turned their heads, and their surprise was so great, that, for a moment, they stood, as it were, bewildered. In another moment, volleys of shot and showers of arrows were sent flying after the fugitive. They flew over his head and whizzed past him, but he heeded them not. Suddenly he turned, and in an oblique line, galloped straight towards the advancing Greeks. More than a dozen Turks, on fleet Arab steeds, were in pursuit, but the Greek was out of their reach. Onward he flew, as though borne by the wind, his ringlets gracefully floating in the breeze. His friends had noticed him. In an instant their arrows flew against his pursuers, who dared advance no further, and, with rage within their hearts, abandoned the chase. Dimitrios had been recognized, and, amid a roaring outburst of applause, he reached the ranks of his countrymen, and, in another moment, the Emperor had embraced him, as though he were a long lost son.

CHAPTER XVI.

Dimitrios had scarcely reached the ranks than he entreated the Emperor to allow him to take part in the fray. Unmindful of the danger from which he had just escaped, his ardent nature spurred him on to cast himself into the midst of new perils. His armor had been taken from him in the Turkish camp, and he wore nothing save the few pieces of clothing that had been left him and an old garment that Selim had obtained for him. The Emperor would not hear of the proposition, and sternly commanded him to return to the city, with a guard of horsemen whom he detailed to accompany him. Obedient to the commands of his Sovereign, but with disappointment in his heart, Dimitrios turned his horse's head toward the city. However, the thought of so soon meeting his sister consoled him. He had proceeded half way, when his curiosity impelled him to turn. Clouds of smoke and dust filled the air, loud shouts could be heard in the distance, swords were flashing right and left over the heads of the soldiers. The Greeks and Turks were in a close engagement. Dimitrios and his companions halted, they could not proceed on their way while Grecian blood was flowing like water. Gladly would our hero have rushed back to take part in the encounter, but the positive command of his master held him to the spot. His eyes were riveted upon the combatants and the fire that sparkled from them was sufficient evidence of what was passing in his heart. At that distance, it was almost impossible to distinguish the Greeks from their enemies, except by their position. The battle-field seemed to be one seething mass of humanity. Evidently the Greeks were endeavoring to force back their enemies upon the great battery which was now silent, for, although the latter were more numerous, they wore little or no armor, and they found themselver unable to withstand the ponderous weapons of the Greeks. For a moment the Turks fell back; the Greeks, profiting by every inch of ground yielded to them, advanced. Dimitrios, perceiving this, could not refrain from exclaiming:

"Bravo! my brave brothers, onward for Christ and Byzantium!"

His enthusiasm, however, was but momentary, for, lo! Turks innumerable were advancing in the rear and on the flanks of their comrades. The ranks of the enemy opened by a sudden movement, so that the way to the coveted battery lay clear before the Greeks.

"Dimitrios," exclaimed one of the veterans who stood beside him, "it is a fearful ruse. Nothing can save our brave men against such frightful odds but a hasty retreat. If the Greeks, flushed by their first successes, advance, the Turks will certainly close in their rear, and, thus hemmed in, the Emperor and every man will perish."

The speaker forgot how hard it was to conquer Greeks by ruse or stratagem.

"See!" cried out Dimitrios, "they are fast retreating, with the Turks following. See our brave cavalry, how it protects the flanks, striking right and left into the enemy. Let us not abide here, the Emperor would be displeased."

Turning their horses, they galloped off towards the

city. Before the ditch they halted. The Greeks were still retreating, followed by the triumphant Turks. They had approached near to the city. It was a ruse on the part of the former. Suddenly the Byzantines make a stand. The Turks, surprised, fall back an instant. The combat begins anew. Far in the rear of the opposing hosts, huge columns of the enemy are moving forward, to assist the vanguard. But, lo! fiery serpents are seen to wing their way through the air from the walls of the city; they fall upon the terrified foeman. The Turkish ranks are broken; for a moment the utmost confusion prevails among the enemy. A wild shout is heard to the left, Dimitrios turns his head, the standard of Venice is fluttering in the breeze.

"God wills it, advance!" sounds over the din of battle, and the old war-cry of the Crusaders seems to animate the Venetians with superhuman ardor. Though only a few hundred men strong, they advance to meet the veterans of Mahomet, followed by a thousand Greeks, who, like themselves, have issued forth from the nearest gate to the south. Few men remain upon the land wall, most of the others are engaged on the side of the Propontis.

The Turks, perceiving the new comers, divided their forces in the van, but the vacant space was immediately filled by the onrushing columns from the rear. It was impossible to withstand the increasing numbers of the enemy. The Venetians fought like lions. At their head, a man of giant form was dealing deadly blows upon the heads of the infidels, his sword fell right and left, claiming countless victims on either side.

"It is Morosini!" exclaimed Dimitrios, who knew the armor of his friend, "Morosini! I never knew he was such a lion. The gentle, philosophical Morosini, what a hero!"

He would have flown to the assistance of his friend, had not the command of the Emperor kept ringing in his ears. Meanwhile, the deadly Greek fire was doing its work, penetrating through the openings in the armor of those who were thus protected, inflicting inexpressible torture and consuming those who were unarmored. But all was unavailing against the overwhelming numbers of the Turks. The Christians, seeing the impossibility of keeping up the unequal contest, slowly retreated toward the walls with their faces to the enemy, in order to afford an opportunity to the Greek cannon and fire to thin their ranks. The Turks, seeing that they were being drawn further from their camp, halted and began their retreat. The battle was at an end. The ground was strewn with the dead and the dying, heartrending shrieks of agony filled the air, broken swords and helmets lay scattered in all directions. The wounded might not be forgotten. There was, perhaps, no nation in mediaeval times which was so solicitous for its wounded as Byzantium. A corps of surgeons and ambulances was never wanting, and the bearer company received a gold piece for every disabled soldier whom it brought off the field after a battle that had been lost. On this occasion, in the midst of the fight, the surgeons and ambulances might be seen moving among the combatants, carrying off, as soon as possible, every wounded man to the rear, and when the Greeks retreated, the disabled were placed in the centre and thus protected, so that few, if any, fell into the hands of the Turks. Now that the fight was over, the wounded were all removed into the city. Dimitrios and his companions had crossed the bridge and entered the gate of Polyandrion as soon as it became evident that the battle was at an end, for he feared the displeasure of the Emperor if he should be found outside the walls.

Instead of immediately returning to his home, he proceeded to the gate, where he knew Morosini would enter. He had but a short time to wait, when the Venetians rushed in. Morosini did not observe his friend, until the latter rode up to him, calling him by name.

"Great Heavens! Dimitrios, have you fallen from the skies?"

"No, my hero, you would better ask if I have risen from the ground, for have I not been buried in the captivity of the Turks?"

"And who broke your bands, reckless boy?"

"I effected my escape, but I will tell you later. How is Helena?"

"Dimitrios, this will be the happiest day of poor Helena's life. She has pined away ever since your sudden disappearance, and had she not received your letter, I fear the worst would have occurred. As it is, she is still very weak."

"Vincent, I can not return home in this guise, will you not procure me clothing?"

"Certainly, friend, go to the Hebdomon, I will send you all you need."

"Those Turkish brutes stole my beautiful armor that had newly been made."

"Never mind your armor, thank God and the Madonna that your life has been saved."

"Has Nicolaus been found?"

"No; the rascal has completely disappeared. The city has been searched in all directions, but all was fruitless. It is all the same now, you are home again."

"Home again," repeated Dimitrios, with a tone of sadness in his voice, "but, alas! for how long?"

"Drive away those sad reflections, Dimitrios, and leave the future to God."

"Farewell, my friend," answered the Greek, and he galloped off towards the palace.

Within an hour, Morosini and his friend were standing before the door of the latter's house. The heart of Dimitrios beat violently, for, though he was rejoiced at the thought of meeting Helena, he could not restrain a certain feeling of fear and a presentiment of ill, which frequently takes possession of a nervous temperament like his. They enter the portal. How familiar is the scene! The events of the past few days seem like a dream. There stands the fountain scattering the spray of its cool water in all directions, beside it is the marble seat upon which Dimitrios and his sister reposed on the morning when the life of Nicolaus Lecapenos seemed to hang suspended on an uncertain thread, the will of the Emperor. Suddenly the door opens. It is Helena! How pale and wan since last we met her! She sees Dimitrios, and with a cry of joy, she rushes towards him. Another moment, and brother and sister are locked in close embrace.

"O! my brother," she exclaimed, "my lost brother, God has brought thee back to me. How can I ever thank Him? How couldst thou be so reckless? I have learned all from thy letter, but what suspense and anxiety did my soul pass through, until that blessed message of joy reached me!"

"My sister," said Dimitrios, gently disengaging himself from her embrace, "your health has suffered much, I see; but you will soon recover; let us thank God that

He who delivered Daniel from the lions' den, has deigned to save me from the cruelty of the Turks. But, alas! poor Irene! where is Irene? Helena, day and night her image haunts me, and my heart is harassed by fear."

"Calm your anxiety, dearest brother, for I have the firm confidence that the Almighty Power of Him who protected you in the midst of peril, will suffer no harm to befall Irene."

Morosini, having now beheld the happy re-union of brother and sister, deemed fit to retire in order not to encroach upon their joy. Divining his intention, Helena exclaimed:

"Morosini, do not leave us. You are now one of the family, you have been to me a second brother, stay and share our happiness." . . . . . .

It was evening. The exciting day was over, and the red glow of sunset illuminated the western horizon, as Morosini, having excused himself on the plea of urgent business, left Dimitrios and Helena to each other's society. The deadly combat had caused a lull in the bombardment, and Constantinople seemed to breathe more freely, though in many a home there was sadness and grief for the dead that had fallen. More than one heart was breaking as the sun sank to rest at the end of a day which long since has been blotted from the pages of history, but which then stood marked in letters of blood, upon the tablets of Byzantium's memory. More than one young widow shed tears that evening for the husband that would never return, and the babe, as it nestled close to the aching breast of its mother, slept soundly in the blissful unconsciousness that war had rendered it fatherless. The aged father knelt beside the bier of him, whom, years before, he had cradled on his knee, but who, cut down in the flower of his manhood, had preceded him to the silent grave, though he had fallen for his country's sake, fallen as heroes fall. The mother, greater than whose love there is no earthly love, gazed with tear-stained eyes upon the face of the boy she had nurtured in his infancy, having given him his life mid dire sufferings, upon the face of the son, once a babe, whom she had fed with her milk. But, O cruel death! thou tyrant of the human race, thou avenger of the first injury inflicted by man upon the Deity, thou hast conquered; there lies thy victim! There lies a flower from one of old Byzantium's trees; its young heart has ceased to beat, no more doth glow within its veins the fervor of Byzantium's blood, but weep not, mother, for the dead, for greater ills await the living. Thy son has fallen, but on earth his sorrows are ended. See you not how calm and peaceful is his brow in death? Weep rather, mother, weep for thy living ones, weep for thyself, weep for the babe still unborn, for Byzantium's doom is sealed.

CHAPTER XVII.

Several days had elapsed since the return of Dimitrios to his home. The siege had been carried on with increased vigor by the Turks, who were daily approaching nearer to the ill-fated city. Their cannon continued to pour massive stones against the walls, which, in several places, began to give signs of yielding. The cannon of the defenders of the city grew more useless as time went on, on account of the increasing weakness of the walls. The end could not be doubtful. The Sultan, assured of victory, absolutely refused to listen to any terms; nothing could satisfy him but the complete possession of Constantinople. Still, the Emperor, aided by Giustiniani, did all he could to protract the siege. They led sorties against the enemy, but it was like endeavoring to hold back the waves of the ocean. They organized attacks by water, but it was evident that nothing could save Constantinople. A dark cloud of gloom was descending over the inhabitants, though some, especially the enemies of the Emperor, seemed to take their fate lightly. Had they not said that they preferred the turban of the Turk to the tiara of the Pope?

Not a day passed without Morosini and Dimitrios seeing each other. Helena had gradually recovered her strength, feeling happy in the thought that her brother was near. Dimitrios and his bosom friend were pacing up and down on a terrace near the southern walls of the city, engaged in deep conversation.

"Yes, Dimitrios," said the Venetian, "it is perfectly true that human passion was the sole cause of the schism. Had there not been an unreasonable ambition in the breasts of the Greeks, you might still be subject to the Pope, as your fathers were."

"I have told you, Vincent, that I will readily admit that a certain primacy of honor had been developed in the Church in favor of the Bishop of Rome, a primacy which was acknowledged both by the East and the West, even by the Œcumenical Patriarch, but I do not see that this primacy was one of jurisdiction."

"My dear Dimitrios, the very fact of the intervention of the Sovereign Pontiff being invoked in grave matters, the very fact of there being an appeal to him against the decision of the Bishops, the fact that his legates presided at the councils, the words of the Fathers of Chalcedon and many other facts prove that Rome exercised jurisdiction over all the Churches."

"Even this," answered the Greek, "may have owed its origin to spontaneous growth. It is not evident to my mind that it was founded upon divine right."

"Do you not know, Dimitrios, that Christ said that He was to build His Church upon a rock? Now the Fathers of the first five centuries all agree in applying this figure to St. Peter, to whom the words are addressed, so that they consider St. Peter as the foundation of the Church. Was it not natural that Christ, having founded His Church, should give to it a head? But what is a head without authority? All tends to prove that St. Peter was the first of the Apostles, therefore he must have been the head of the Church, for he was the first among the first. Even a heathen writer of the fourth century, with whom you are, no doubt, acquainted, I mean Ammianus Marcellinus, tells us that the supreme authority over the Christians was vested in the Bishop of Rome. St. Cyprian, in one of his epistles to St. Cornelius, says that the Church was founded upon Peter, and he writes that to be in communion with the Bishop of Rome, is equivalent to being in communion with the Catholic Church."

"If that is the case," answered Dimitrios, "we, poor Greeks, are badly off, for we are separated from the unity of the Church. But, leaving this question for the present,—for I intend to study it myself,—allow me to ask you another, one connected with discipline. Why is it that the Latin Priests are forbidden to marry?"

Morosini smiled.

"This is a peculiar question," he said, "and it seems to have little to do with the Primacy, but I will answer it. You admit that a life of absolute continence is better than marriage, for your own monks and nuns are bound to it for life, and your Bishops are celibates. Acting on this principle, the Church has, from the earliest times, both in the East and the West, forbidden persons in Holy Orders to marry, as is evident from the councils of Neocaesarea and Nicaea. About the year 305, it was decreed in the West, in the council of Elvira, that the ministers of the Church should live in continence, even if they had been married before ordination. This law held good only for the West, and did not prevail in the East, as the council of Nicaea refused to impose it upon the whole Church. It appears, though, that about the middle of the fifth century, the law of celibacy, which existed among the Latins, prevailed, also, in certain parts of Greece, namely Thessaly, Macedonia and Achaia. It rarely happened that a Bishop was married, but the synod in Trullo required him, if married, to separate from his wife, and forbade all clerics to marry after the sub-diaconate. Leo the Wise, in the ninth century, modified this law and permitted sub-deacons, deacons and priests who had married after taking orders to remain in the ranks of the clergy, without, however, exercising sacred functions. Remember, this was in your own Constantinople. These practises finally developed into the present practise of the Greek Church, namely, that Bishops cannot be married, that no cleric may marry after being ordained deacon, and that, although those who were married before ordination may continue to live in the marriage state, they cannot marry a second time, after the death of their wives. Thus you see that celibacy truly exists among the Greeks, but only in a modified form. Are you satisfied?"

"Perfectly," answered Dimitrios, "you have rendered the matter clear. I thank you. Really, Morosini, you ought to have been a priest, you are so versed in theology and ecclesiastical history, although I would not have said so when I saw you cutting off the heads of the Turks not long ago."

"We are not all called to that sublime vocation, my friend—there are various degrees in the Church, and it is necessary that all positions should be filled."

As in walking up and down, they turned toward the sea, Morosini suddenly stopped, and, taking Dimitrios by the arm, said:

"Do you see those vessels in the distance? They are bearing this way, and are evidently coming from the Hellespont, with all sail set. Behold! they are firing cannon; see the smoke as it suddenly bursts forth; they are pursuing an enemy."

"They must be friends," exclaimed Dimitrios, "if they are firing upon the Turks, for there are no other ships to fire upon, while these waters are filled with Turkish ships."

It could be distinctly seen that there was a distant naval engagement, although the sound of cannon could not be heard, it being drowned by the greater noise caused by the firing which was kept up in the vicinity of the city. The ships, however, drew nearer, for their sails were filled with a favorable breeze. They were firing broadsides as they advanced, while it was evident that there was some defect in their enemies, who seemed to be firing at random.

"I can see distinctly," said Morosini, "they are five, and they are following one another in a line. Look! do you notice that large vessel to the right? it is sinking; the balls of the newcomers have taken effect."

The ship indicated was evidently going down; it could be seen to settle, when, suddenly, plunging head foremost, it disappeared beneath the waves.

"There is one of the infidel ships gone!" said Morosini.

The strangers plowed the waves, dividing the waters as they sped onward. The Greek ships in the Golden Horn had noticed their arrival, for they redoubled their energy in firing upon every Turkish vessel within range of their guns.

"Another one is sinking," exclaimed Dimitrios, "do you see that huge craft yonder? Its days are numbered."

The old ship sank from sight, and still another, and another was disabled, two were set on fire, but the newcomers seemed to suffer nothing. They were now in the midst of the Turkish fleet, but still they flew onward, wafted by the breeze, and firing as they went. Not only balls of stone were hurled against the wooden hulks of the infidels, but the dreaded Greek fire flew right and left among the fleet of the enemy, carrying death and terror into their hearts, and causing them, as it were, under the influence of a panic fear, to fly for their lives. The five ships had forced their way through the Turkish fleet, and they were now under the walls of Constantinople. A loud cry of joy and welcome arose from the ranks of the city's defenders, a demonstration in which both Dimitrios and Morosini joined with heartfelt gladness. It was answered from the decks of the ships.

"I told you they were friends," said Dimitrios, "whence can they have come? One is flying the standard of Constantinople, but what are the other colors?"

Dimitrios pointed to the ships, and Morosini replied: "It is the flag of Genoa, I think."

"Whatever they are," said Dimitrios, "they have performed a brave deed. In spite of Turkish ships and Turkish cannon, they have reached the Golden Horn in safety."

Indeed, the five vessels were just entering the harbor, the chain having been lowered to allow them to pass, and, as they sailed triumphantly into the Golden Horn, they were greeted by prolonged cheers from the decks of the Greek vessels, as well as from the shore. A great and heroic deed had been performed. The news soon spread from one end of the city to the other; it went from mouth to mouth, as usually, growing as it grew older, assuming gigantic proportions, and raising the spirits of the Greeks.

As Morosini and his friend descended into the streets of the city, they were greeted on all sides by questions such as these: "Have you heard the news?" "Did you see the ships?" "Is it true that the Turkish fleet has been burned?" Or, information was vouchsafed to them in this form: "We are saved; Venice and Genoa have sent us a combined fleet of fifty galleys each; they have sunk a number of Turkish vessels, and are now scouring the Bosphorous and the Propontis."

"Would to God it were true!" answered Dimitrios to one who brought him this wonderful piece of news, but, alas! my friend, you have been misinformed."

"What! have no ships come to our assistance? I was informed by one who had seen them."

"That may be true, but he certainly did not see more than five, except it be ships of the enemy."

When the real state of affairs became known, and the excitement had somewhat subsided, it was learned that the five ships, with their heroic crews, had come from the Ægean Sea. The effect of this arrival was, for a brief period, to revive the drooping spirits of the Greeks. But this was like the last flickering of a candle about to be extinguished.

"I am rejoiced," said Morosini to Dimitrios, "that the ships have come, but they will not avail to save us. The numbers of our enemies are overwhelming. We may hold out a few weeks longer, but the unfortunate city is doomed; nothing can save us now except a powerful intervention of the West, or a miraculous assistance from on high."

CHAPTER XVIII.

Easter had come and gone. The ceremonies of Holy Week, performed according to the elaborate ritual of the Greek Church, had never been more impressive. It seemed as though Constantinople was anticipating its own crucifixion by a Gethsemane of fearful anticipation. A damper was thrown over the joys of Easter, which all felt would be the last celebrated under the dome of St Sophia. Only a few Greeks had participated in the celebration within the walls of that glorious temple, for the populace and the inferior clergy, together with the monks, could not be reconciled to the thought that the Pope's authority was again received in Constantinople, and its principal church.

A singular circumstance had occurred on Easter morning, which had produced a strong impression upon the sensitive heart of Dimitrios. At the moment that he was leaving St. Sophia, after assisting at Mass, a man of wild aspect, with flaming eyes, was standing at the western entrance, exclaiming in a solemn voice: "Woe to Constantinople!" Continuing, he cited the words of the prophet: "Declare ye among the nations, and publish it; lift up a standard, proclaim and conceal it not; say: Babylon is taken . . . . for a nation is come up against her out of the North, which shall make her land desolate. My people hath been a lost flock; their shepherds have caused them to go astray. Remove out of the midst of Babylon . . . . Her foundations are fallen; her walls are thrown down, for it is the vengeance of the Lord .... Woe to them, for their day is come, the time of their visitation .... At the noise of the taking of Babylon, the earth is moved, and the cry is heard among the nations."

A crowd had gathered around the speaker, and they listened to him in the most profound silence; his words seemed prophetic; he appeared inspired. Proceeding in the same strain, but no longer using the words of Scripture, he spoke thus, with his eyes raised heavenward:

"Thus spoke the Prophet concerning Babylon, and thus speak I concerning thee, O, city of Constantine! thou Constantinople of to-day, and Constantinople of centuries hence; for what is done to thee now, shall be repeated in ages to come, when the besiegers shall be besieged. As the Empire of Constantine has fallen to pieces, thus shall the Empire of Mahomet crumble. In the South the children of Greece shall arise, and the children of the Prophet shall be confounded and put to flight; in the North, the provinces shall free themselves from the yoke. Then shall a nation come upon thee, O, Constantinople! from the North; a nation that shall devour thee. That shall be the day of revenge. Then shall once more sounds of rejoicing be heard within the walls of St. Sophia, and the Empire of Constantine be restored."

The strange being ceased speaking, and, without addressing a word to any one, he wrapped his cloak around him and walked away; no one knew whither he had gone.

Several weeks had passed since then; the siege had

been carried on with increasing activity on the part
of the Turks, who were now nearly under the walls, in
spite of the Greek fire which was poured into their ranks
by the besieged. They had their engines of war into
position, using catapults, which cast huge blocks of
stone among their enemies, while their cannon continued to batter the walls, which had given away in
several places. Battering rams stood ready to be
used in case the opportunity presented itself, and a
number of scaling ladders were at hand. The loss of
the Turks was considerable, but, as fast as they fell,
others immediately took their place, either at the cannon, the formidable mortars which wrought dire havoc
among the besieged, the catapults, or among the archers.

Constantine had made a last appeal to Mahomet in
behalf of his capital, offering to submit to him and pay
any tribute he might desire. It was not cowardice
which prompted him to this step, but rather a wish to
save the population from massacre and pillage, which,
he knew, would be inevitable in case the city were carried by storm. But all was in vain; the young monarch of the Turks, flushed with victory, rejected the
proposition with scorn. For Constantine there remained
naught save—to die.

The month of May was hastening to its close. Dimitrios and Morosini had both spent a sleepless night upon
the walls. The morning found them together on the
grounds of the old Imperial Palace. The sun had not
yet risen, but at that season of the year it was already
broad daylight. The Eastern sky, adorned with the
roseate hue of the morning, announced that the glorious
orb would soon burst forth in all its splendor.

"My friend," said Morosini, sadly, "all may be considered lost; the Turks have gained possession of the Golden Horn."

"What a gigantic undertaking!" replied the young Greek. "Yes, who would have dreamt of it? In one single night they have launched at least a hundred vessels in the inner harbor."

"But I cannot see how they could possibly have done it."

"By dint of labor. You know that Mahomet caused a passage of nearly two leagues to be dug over land beyond Pera. This he lined with planks smeared with grease. His vessels were placed upon rollers, and these, by means of engines and a multitude of men, were dragged from the Bosphorus into the Golden Horn."

"A stroke of genius, worthy of a better cause!" exclaimed Dimitrios.

"But this is not all," said Morosini, "three great breaches are appearing in the walls; the first between the Palace of the Hebdomon and the Gate of Polyandrion; the second near the Gate of Charisius, and the third between the Gate Roussion and the Selymbria Gate. Our brave men are posted at each of these weak spots; they will fight like lions, I know, but numbers will overwhelm them."

"Ah! Morosini, hard days are before us. Shall we ever meet again in peaceful conversation? Who knows? Our dead bodies shall, perhaps, soon lie side by side. I have thought seriously over the question of the Papacy. Helena and myself have conversed on the subject, and I find that, long before I had thought of it, she had given the matter earnest consideration. I found her determined to be reconciled with the Latin Church, and she entreated me to follow her example. I have prayed long and fervently; light has succeeded to darkness, I believe. I would not dare to die in schism. I see now clearly that the Church of Christ is one, one in doctrine and one in government. I see that the Pope is the historical successor of St. Peter, and that it was to Peter that Christ gave authority to feed His lambs and His sheep. Christian antiquity shows me clearly that those who were not in communion with the successors of Peter, were looked upon as heretics and schismatics. If I enter into communion with Rome, I must believe as Rome believes, for Christ prayed for Peter, that his faith might not fail. He told him to confirm his brethren and the doctrine of the Church is one. Moreover, there must be a centre of truth and a centre of unity and this, I am convinced, is nowhere to be found but in Peter and his successors. I am now decided, all steps have been taken, the Emperor is delighted, and, on this very day, I will be reconciled to the Church of our Fathers by the Papal Legate himself. Helena will kneel at my side to abjure the schism."

"O, Dimitrios!" exclaimed Morosini, taking both the hands of his friend, "how can I congratulate you? This is, indeed, the happiest day of my life. Now can I die in peace, for I know that the prodigal has returned home."

Although Morosini was, by no means, a man of sentiment, he could not restrain, nor did he attempt to conceal, the tears that were trickling down his cheeks. They were tears of joy over the return of an innocent wanderer to the mother he had despised because he had not known her.

"I feel happy," he went on, "because now I will know that you and Helena are safe."

"Poor Helena!" said Dimitrios, "what will become of her?"

"As to Helena," replied Morosini, "as long as my hand can wield a sword, she shall be protected; if that fails"—the Italian pointed upward—"there liveth and reigneth One who rules the world; trust in Him."

"Shall we leave Helena at home?"

"What better place of safety can you find? My vigilant eyes shall be ever upon that house. You know my position. I am perfectly free. The handful of Venetians under my command are in my pay. I am subject to none, having volunteered my services in behalf of the Empire. My lieutenant is as well able to conduct my little company as I am myself. I will be everywhere at once—guards will be stationed at your house, and a swift courier, who will apprise me at the first approach of danger."

"But what will you be able to do in the midst of the confusion, when the city is taken by storm?"

"Leave that to me. Do you not confide in your friend?"

"As much as in myself, Vincent."

The cannonading was terrific. From all sides a heavy fire was being poured into the unfortunate city. All the batteries on the land side were playing against the tottering walls, while a number of mortars were casting heavy stones upon the besieged. The Turkish ships in the Golden Horn as well as those upon the waters of the Propontis, united their efforts with those of the army. It was now certain that Constantinople would soon be in the power of the Infidel.

Mahomet, to urge on his troops, promised them the spoil. "The city and the buildings," he had said, "are mine; but I resign to you the captives and the spoil, the treasures of gold and beauty; be rich, and be happy." Nothing more was needed to spur on men, thirsting for Christian blood and Christian riches, and already rendered impatient by the protracted siege and the stubborn resistance of the Greeks. They worked with a will at the cannon.

While the Turkish cannon roared, announcing the approaching end, the day wore on. The evening was approaching. Dimitrios and Helena had both been reconciled to the Church of Rome, their hearts, as well as the heart of Morosini, were filled with peace and happiness, in spite of the awful fate that seemed impending. As the shades of night began to fall upon the doomed city, the cannonading gradually ceased, until it was finally succeeded by an ominous silence, which, all felt, was the calm that preceded the storm.

The Emperor had summoned Dimitrios and Morosini to his presence, in the Blachernae Palace. Alas! it was the last time they would meet there.

As the two friends entered into the presence of the Sovereign, they found him standing with his arms crossed upon his breast. His face wore an expression of deep agony, his furrowed brow, and the lines upon his countenance bespoke the strain of mental anguish that had been laid upon him. As his glance fell upon the two faithful subjects, his eye brightened and a sad smile formed itself upon his face. They knelt before him, he bade them rise. Embracing Dimitrios, he spoke:

"My dearest son, once more receive the sincere congratulations of Constantine, the last Emperor of Byzantium. Thou art now my brother indeed, a son of Holy Church, our common Mother."

The tender-hearted youth, heedless of the Imperial dignity, leaned his head upon the Emperor's shoulder, and wept. Morosini could not restrain his tears. The scene was touching. There stood the last scion of the Imperial House of Paleologos, the last successor of Constantine the Great, Constantine XI. His eyes were dimmed with tears. In his arms he clasped a noble descendant of a family that had once wielded the scepter over the Byzantine Empire. That scepter was broken, the crown was about to fall forever, the Imperial Eagle was dying.

"O, Dimitrios! how joyful and yet how sad!" spoke the Monarch, "joyful to think that we die in the Church of Christ, and yet sad to leave our children in the hands of the enemy. I feel the shadows of death fast gathering around me; my son, we soon must part. I feel that Constantine soon must die, but his death shall be the death of the brave. Blessed are the dead that die in the Lord! But, Oh, how frightful the fate of the living! My heart is pierced with anguish when I think of the doom of this fair city."

The Emperor's voice faltered, it was choked with his sobs. A silence succeeded, more painful than words. The hearts of the three men seemed to melt into one. Dimitrios and Morosini both knelt before their Sovereign, they kissed his hands.

"My children," said the Emperor, "farewell! We shall meet upon the field of battle, and then——"

Pointing his hand upward, he added:

"And then, beyond the skies."

He could speak no more. Casting a last, loving glance upon those he had loved so well and who had proved themselves faithful to the end, Constantine withdrew.

Dark night fell upon Byzantium's walls, silence reigned supreme.

CHAPTER XIX.

The dreary night was at an end. Before the break of day, the Emperor and his guard stood beside the gate of St. Romanus, where the principal breach was yawning to allow the entrance of the foe. Two towers had been leveled by the Ottoman cannon, and the debris filled the ditch. Guistiniani was there with the men of Genoa, and there too, stood Morosini with his brave Venetian volunteers. Dimitrios, clad from head to foot in armor, grasped his sword nervously, while his eyes remained fixed upon the Emperor.

Within the city, the inhabitants were filled with dismay, many spending hours in the churches, to implore the help of God. Dimitrios had given strict orders to Helena not to leave the house, before which several Venetian guards were stationed in accordance with the promise of Morosini.

When the first streaks of dawn announced the end of the night, the roar of Turkish cannon ushered in the day. On all sides of the unfortunate city, the awful peals of warlike thunder rent the air. Still the brave defenders stood at their post. Mid fear and anxiety the day wore on. Constantinople was still in possession of its rightful owners. At night, the fire of artillery ceased, but Constantine and his followers remained at their post, guarding the dangerous breach. Sleep had fled from the eyes of the inhabitants, no one knew what the morrow might bring forth. Dimitrios hastily partook of a slight refreshment, though his appetite had forsaken him, for he knew that the struggle of life and death was about to commence.

The Turkish army was drawn up on the other side of the ditch, along the land wall. It resembled a bloodthirsty tiger, crouching, in order to spring upon its prey.

Slowly the weary hours wore on, there was no change in the situation. The hour of midnight finally arrived. It began the last day of the Byzantine Empire, the memorable 29th of May, of the year 1453.

A soldier approached Dimitrios.—

"The Emperor wishes you to come to him," said the man. The youth immediately obeyed the summons, and, proceeding to the spot where the Sovereign of Byzantium stood, he found Morosini standing beside him.

"Dimitrios," said the Monarch, "we have loved each other in life, we shall love each other in death. I now proceed to St. Sophia. I feel that it is for the last time. Morosini goes with me. Will you accompany us?"

"My heart overflows with gratitude towards you, my Sovereign, at the thought of the honor conferred upon your humble servant, to bear you company at this most solemn moment."

"I will partake of the Body of the Lord, will you too strengthen yourself with the Sacrament, which, as St. Chrysostom says, makes men strong as lions?"

"I will, most serene lord, for it may be for us the Viaticum."

"Come then, my faithful friends."

The Emperor mounted his horse, and his companions following his example, they rode off towards the church in which the Christian mysteries were to be celebrated for the last time. Without, all was plunged in the thickest darkness, broken only by the torches carried by the attendants of the Emperor, but the sacred edifice was in a blaze of light. Numerous lamps in which perfumed oil fed the flame, were everywhere suspended, casting a golden reflection upon the marble and the splendid mosaics of the interior. Never did St. Sophia seem so solemn. A multitude had gathered within it, in spite of the early hour and the fact that the Sacred Mysteries were to be celebrated according to the Latin rite. The awful solemnity of the moment seemed to have suppressed the animosity of the Greeks against the Latin Church. Women were sobbing, while strong men, with solemn faces, stood looking upon the awe-inspiring scene.

The Emperor had occupied his stall, and he kept Dimitrios and Morosini near him. At the altar stood a priest, clad in the vestments of the Latin Church. A Roman Cardinal, the envoy of the Sovereign Pontiff, was also there, besides high dignitaries of the Greek Church. They had all spent a sleepless night in anticipation of the awful fate that was impending.

The Sacred Mysteries were offered up. At the moment of the Holy Communion, the Emperor approached the altar. The deepest recollection was pictured in his countenance. He fell upon his knees before the priest, he raised his eyes and fixed them upon the Sacred Host; there was something in them which was not of the earth. A sweet feeling of peace came over the soul of Constantine which mirrored itself in his features. The voice of the celebrant re-echoed at that solemn hour, under the lofty dome and through the aisles of St. Sophia: "May the Body of our Lord Jesus Christ preserve thy soul unto eternal life!" *For the last time!* Words such as these rang in the ears of Dimitrios. "For the last time! Tomorrow it will be the name of Mahomet."

The Byzantine Emperor had partaken of the Sacrament of the Eucharist in the Church of Justinian. He arose and returned to his seat, to the west of the Sacred edifice, facing the altar. Dimitrios and Morosini also received the Holy Communion.

Mass was over, but the people still remained. After a prayer of thanksgiving, the Emperor arose, bent his knee before the altar, and, beckoning to Morosini and Dimitrios to follow him, departed. As they left the Church, a piercing cry was heard at the distance of a few yards before them, and a man in long robes and hands upraised to heaven, darted away, disappearing in the darkness.

"Woe! woe!" he cried, "woe to Constantinople!"

The Emperor, summoning one of his attendants, bade him run after the strange individual, fearing lest his cries might excite a panic among the population. Again the cry resounded:

"Woe to Constantinople; woe to Byzantium; woe to Constantine!"

All was silent once more, the man had vanished.

"It is the same person," said Dimitrios, "who, on Easter Sunday, attracted attention by his singular words on this very spot."

"Alas!" replied the Emperor, "his words are awful, but I fear that they truly indicate the tragic end of the Queen of Cities. My friends, I leave you now to snatch a few moments' repose which I badly need. Tomorrow I will need it no longer. Farewell, once more, Vincent, may God's blessing rest upon you for your fidelity to Constantine Paleologus! farewell, Dimitrios, my cherished youth, may God's holy angels guard you! Farewell, my friends, until we meet in the Bosom of God."

The Sovereign of Byzantium embraced for the last time the two faithful servants, whom he loved as though they were his equals, and, with sorrow in his soul, departed towards the half-ruined Palace, where so many Emperors of Byzantium had slept before him. Constantine soon fell into blissful unconsciousness, and the last of the Emperors slept his last sleep upon earth.

Dimitrios and Morosini, knowing that they would stand in need of all their strength, concluded to follow the Sovereign's example and retired to the quarters of the guards within the enclosure of the Palace, where they snatched a few hours' sleep. They were up before the sun, and while darkness still covered the earth. They enquired whether the Emperor had yet left the Palace, and learned that thus far, he had not been seen. Hereupon they proceeded through the Royal Gate, where a crowd had already gathered, and where a richly caparisoned horse was held in readiness for the Emperor.

The horses of the two friends were also saddled. They had not long to wait, for a tramp of feet within the walls announced that the attendants of the sovereign were approaching. In a few moments the Emperor, careworn and sad, made his appearance. Dimitrios and Morosini knelt before him, kissing his hands. The crowd drew back in mournful silence. The Emperor mounted his horse. His ministers and the members of his household crowded around him for a last farewell. Constantine, holding the reins in his left hand, and raising the right, made a motion that he was about to speak. The multitude awaited his words in breathless attention.

"My children," thus sounded his voice amid the silence of that awful morning, "my children, the end has come. Death shall find your sovereign fighting in defence of a city he may not save, but"—here the monarch raised his voice—"of a city—let it be handed down to posterity—of a city he has loved until his latest breath."

Suppressed sobs, bursting from the breasts of the spectators, were wafted upon the morning air. The Emperor continued:

"Yea, I have loved Byzantium, the fair city of Constantine, the city that bears a name I bear; I have loved Byzantium, loved it to the end; for Byzantium I have lived; for Byzantium I die."

Loud wailing arose from the lips of the multitude; women shrieked, warriors, grown grey upon the battlefield, brushed the tears from their eyes.

"Weep not for me, my children, weep rather for yourselves. Weep for Constantinople. Whatever ills betide you, Oh, let your Emperor, with his dying lips, implore you, be true to your country: be true to your God! All men have their faults, Constantine has had his. If I have ever injured any man, it wittingly or unwittingly, I have been the cause that the innocent one has suffered, in this solemn moment of my life, before our common Creator, and in presence of you, my brethren, I beg you all—forgiveness."

Loud sobs and lamentations interrupted this speech.

"Farewell! my children," cried Constantine, and the Emperor rode on to meet his fate. Dimitrios and his Venetian friend sprang into the saddle and followed their master.

High arose, borne aloft by the breeze of the morning, as though a distant echo, the cry: "Woe to Constantinople! Woe to Constantine!" The Emperor heeded it not; his friends were silent. They reached the gate of St. Romanus. The bulk of the little Greek army was there. Besides the Emperor stood Giustiniani, sword in hand. To his left Morosini and his Venetians took up their stand, while Dimitrios occupied his place among the Emperor's guards.

The morn of the 29th of May was dawning. Faint rays from the East shot over the heads of the valiant defenders of Constantinople, reflecting upon the Turkish army before the ditch. Suddenly a shout arose from the thousands of Turkish mouths, and a horde, like an avalanche, heedless of danger and death, precipitated itself upon the walls. A general attack had begun all along the walls at the weak spots, where breaches had been made. The main attack was at the northwestern portion of the wall, where the great breach yawned, beside the gate of St. Romanus. The Greeks filled the outer ramparts. The Turks rushed on, though thousands fell, pierced by the arrows of the city's defenders, or hewn down by their swords. The Greeks fought like lions, the Turks like demons. The ponderous weapons of the former fell thick and fast upon the felt caps and unarmored bodies of the latter. Countless infidels were hurled back into the ditch as they attempted to scale the walls. Shouts of despair, imprecations of the besiegers, cries of the wounded and groans of the dying mingled with the clash of arms. The intrepid Christians struck right and left; they drove back their assailants; it availed naught. Twelve thousand Janizaries stood before them. With flashing sabres in their hands they formed successive columns of attack. Hardly was one repelled, when another took its place. The number of the enemies seemed infinite. Their dead bodies were heaped up in piles; they were fast filling the ditch; still new hordes advanced. The Greeks were fast succumbing to fatigue. Dimitrios, with a shield on his left arm, and a long sword in the right hand, slew right and left, and many a Turk paid dearly for encountering the young Greek in mortal combat. The ditch was now filled with the bodies of the slain. They formed a solid ground under the feet of the Janizaries, who rushed on directly to the attack. The Greeks fell back, impelled by the onrushing forces of the enemy. A huge son of the desert, a Turk, a true Goliath in size, with flaming eyes, raised his scimitar above the head of Constantine. Dimitrios noticed the danger of his sovereign. The blow had fallen, but upon the Emperor's shield. In another moment the infidel lay biting the dust, pierced by the sword of Dimitrios. The Emperor's life was spared, but another illustrious victim had fallen, Giustianiani lay wounded in the face with an arrow. Speedily the bleeding chieftain was carried away by his brave men and taken on board his galley. The ranks of the Christians were sadly thinned, the Emperor and a few companions stood nearly alone, still they yielded not.

A loud cry is heard; there is a fearful rush; onward fly a troop of Janizaries, headed by Hassan of Ulabad. Dimitrios casts a rapid glance around him. Only a few Greeks are visible. Where is Morosini? The Emperor stands there still. But it is all in vain; naught can save him now. His sword still falls upon the heads of the enemy, but he is wounded, covered with blood and exhausted. The Turks rush on; the breach is filled with their numbers. Constantinople is conquered and Constantine Paleologos falls, unknown to his enemies, who rush over his body into the city. All grows dark before the eyes of Dimitrios; he sees no more; he sinks; he falls; Dimitrios Phocas lies prostrate upon the ground. A piercing cry re-echoes over Byzantium's walls: "Woe, woe to Constantine! Woe to Constantinople!" The prophecy has been fulfilled; Byzantium has fallen.

CHAPTER XX.

"Oh, my brother, my brother!" This was the stifled cry which burst from the lips of the sister of Dimitrios, as, now and anon, she arose from her attitude of prayer, to give vent to her feelings.

"Zoe," she said, turning to her old nurse, "tell me, how think you it will end; shall I ever behold him again?"

"Courage, dear lady," replied the faithful servant, "God is good."

The words were spoken in such a hopeless tone, that they brought little consolation with them.

"The firing has nearly ceased," said Helena, "but that ominous sound, like the distant roar of the ocean, bodes no good. Perhaps at this very moment—"

She covered her face with her hands, as if afraid to think what her lips were about to utter.

Hours of intense anxiety had thus worn away, Helena, now lying prostrate in prayer, then seeking relief in the exchange of words with Zoe. From time to time, the old woman would go to the outer door, to inquire from some solitary pedestrian as to the progress of the struggle, but what she heard was far from reassuring. Then she would return to her young mistress and endeavor to cheer her with hopes which she knew were groundless.

Suddenly, loud cries were heard in the distance, as of a multitude rushing onward.

"O, Heavens!" cried Helena, "what does that mean?"

"Be calm, lady," replied Zoe, "I will go and see."

"O, Zoe, be careful, venture not into the streets!"

The latter, without waiting to reply, hastened to the door. She was met by one of the Venitian guards, running breathlessly into the house.

"Noble lady," he exclaimed, "fly, fly quickly, if you value your life; the Turks are upon us!"

The uproar grew louder, and it appeared as though the sound of tumultuous voices proceeded from the street in front of the house. Cries and shrieks of females could be heard above the din.

"Heaven, protect us!" exclaimed Helena.

"Follow me," shouted the Venetian, leading the way.

"Dimitrios, where is Dimitrios? I do not want to live without Dimitrios," shrieked the girl, half crazed with terror. Zoe took her mistress by the hand and dragged her to the door, through which the Venetian had just passed. As they reached the threshold, a horrible sight met their eyes. The unfortunate guard, who had risked his own life to save theirs, lay lifeless upon the ground in a pool of blood; his head had been cleaved by a blow from a Turkish scimiter.

"Ah, here is a prize!" exclaimed a ferocious Turk, as his eyes fell upon the Greek maiden. Though Zoe understood not his words, she divined his intention, as he advanced towards her mistress. Clasping her arms around her, as though she would hide her from the infidel, she cried out:

"Help, mercy, spare her!"

The follower of Mahomet rudely thrust her off, but

still she clung to Helena, who was rendered speechless by fright.

"Begone, hag!" roared the Turk, "this girl is mine. I was the first to lay eyes on her."

The faithful servant held on to her mistress.

"If you will not let go your hold, take that," and the brute severed the head of the unfortunate woman with one blow of his sabre. Scenes similar to this were being enacted in all quarters of constantinople. The sight of this atrocious deed caused the head of Helena to reel; her eyes grew dim—she had fainted. The Musselman caught her as she fell.

"What are you doing, Ali, ugly scarecrow?" exclaimed a young Turk, more than six feet high, "give up that woman, I claim her!"

"She is mine, by right of possession."

"I say she is mine by the right of the strongest, or the right of conquest, if you like; give her up at once."

"I will not, you shall have to fight for her first."

"Look here, Ali, what is the use of friends fighting? We shall compromise the matter. But, fool, the girl is dead!"

"No, she is not, she has only fainted. We will soon revive her."

A sound of horses hoofs is heard; the Turks look around. A rider is rushing on at full speed. The ground groans beneath him; heedlessly he rides over the Turks he encounters, if they are unfortunate enough to fall in his way. No one dares to intercept him, all eyes are turned with wonder toward him. Ali, still holding the unconscious girl in his arms, and the newcomer look bewildered toward the rider. As the latter approaches the two men, he gradually slackens his speed, then, at the distance of a few yards from them, he makes a sign, as if about to speak. They gaze at him in astonishment. Arriving near Ali, as quickly as lightning flashes, he bends over, clasps Helena in his left arm, draws her across the saddle, and darts off like an arrow shot from the bow. The shock received by Ali was so great that the clumsy Turk fell sprawling upon the ground.

"Hold him," he cried, "hold the thief, the dog of a Christian!"

His companion roared with laughter as he beheld the discomfited Ali struggling to his feet. This enraged the brute still more, and he sprang at his neighbor like a tiger.

"This is thy fault, villain!" he exclaimed, "and thou darest laugh at me!"

"Be cool, Ali," said the other, "don't be angry."

"Angry?" roared Ali, "angry? thou hound, I will choke thee!"

"Choke me? Come, Ali, learn better manners than to talk to a comrade about choking. There! I will not choke thee, I will do something else," and the giant placed one arm around Ali's waist, turning him as though he had been a reed, and setting him upon his head, while he held both feet in the air.

"Now, Ali," he inquired, laughing, "are you prepared to choke?"

The unfortunate Ali struggled to free himself, but his friend, or rather enemy then, held him in his iron grasp. The comic spectacle attracted a number of other Turks who had witnessed the proceedings from afar, and, for a moment, forgetting their work of plunder, they ran up to enjoy the fun.

"What is the matter, Ismael?" queried one of their number.

"Nothing of importance. Two ravens happened to catch a beautiful little dove, but an eagle suddenly flew on and snatched the dove away from both. The dove is gone and the ravens are fighting it out between themselves."

"Let me go, for Mahomet's sake," cried Ali, "the blood is rushing to my head."

"Well, I will let thee go, for we are losing our precious time, but if thou ever again dost threaten to choke me, I will not let thee off so easily."

Then he loosed his hold on Ali's feet, and the poor fellow again tumbled on the ground, to the great amusement of the spectators. Ali, red with shame and rage, arose and skulked off, casting upon Ismael a look which, to any one acquainted with the art of reading the human face, would have spoken the language of deep revenge. In the midst of these scenes, the rider and the Greek girl had been forgotton.

No sooner had Morosini, the deliverer of Helena, placed the poor girl upon his saddle, than he galloped off as fast as the fiery steed he rode could carry him. His position was one of extreme danger, for the streets were filled with Turks, and no Greek was safe. Still, it was a matter of life and death, and Morosini sped on his way. He knew that it would be impossible for him to gain the open country beyond the walls, for the Turks were scattered in all directions. There was no thought of entering a house, as the whole city was given up to pillage. His only hope lay in gaining a boat which, by his orders, lay concealed in a remote part of the harbor, and he hoped that the Turks would be so busily engaged in plundering the inhabitants that they would pay little attention to the water front. But how could he possibly reach the boat? At all events, it was necessary to hazard the experiment, so on he flew. He had arrived opposite the Hippodrome on his way to the south-eastern portion of the city, when an arrow came whizzing through the air. It pierced the breast of his steed; the animal tottered and fell over the rider and his charge. In a moment half a dozen Turks surrounded them.

"Hold!" cried a man of Herculean frame, "I brought down the rider; these Greeks are mine. Woe to him who touches a hair of their heads! You know me?"

The Turks drew back.

"Help me to draw away the animal," he added.

A number set to work, and the horse was dragged off. The Turk approached Morosini and said to him in Greek:

"Arise, young man, I did it for your own good. Fear nothing. You and the lady are safe now. Think not of resistance, for it would be your death. I assure you that not a hair of the lady's head shall be hurt. But she has fainted."

Spreading his cloak upon the ground, he said:

"Lay her down here." Then, turning to one of the Turks, he spoke in a tone of authority:

"Fetch some water, immediately."

Kneeling beside the unconscious girl, he gently opened her lips and let fall into her mouth a few drops of a liquid he carried in a small flask by his side. As Morosini at that moment happened to turn his head, he beheld a multitude of people moving in the direction of St. Sophia.

"It is the Sultan," said the Turk, "but fear not, we shall not be molested; you are safe with me."

In the centre of the Hippodrome stood a peculiar monument of venerable antiquity, a three-headed brazen serpent. It had been dedicated at Delphi, in the year 470 B. C. by Pausanias and the Greeks, as a monument of their victory over the Persians at Plataea. Constantine had brought it to Byzantium, on removing the seat of the empire. As Mahomet reached the spot where the Delphic monument stood, he rose in his stirrups and, with one blow of his mace, smote away the jaws of the nearest serpent. Morisini could not refrain from a feeling of indignation at the sight of this wanton deed, and the blood rushed to his head and suffused his cheeks with a crimson tint. The Turk noticed his indignation, and said to him:

"Young man, if you will follow my advice, you will abstain from showing anger at anything you may see." Morosini was silent. Meanwhile, the Turkish soldier returned with the water he had been sent for. Helena seemed to be regaining consciousness. The Venetian, kneeling beside her, succeeded, with some difficulty, in causing her to swallow the liquid. Opening her eyes, she gazed around her as though bewildered, and, with a feeble voice, asked:

"Where am I?"

"You are safe, Helena, and with friends," said Vincent. She gazed at him with a stupified air, as though she did not recognize him and she were seeking to recall some event; finally, she exclaimed with a faint smile:

"Vincent Morosini! Thank Heaven!"

Allowing her eyes to wander around, she added:

"Where is my brother?"

"He will soon return," answered Vincent.

"And Zoe?" inquired the girl. Then, as if the remembrance of the bloody scene she had witnessed shot across her mind, she put her hands before her face, as if to shut out the fearful vision.

"We must remove her from here," said the Turk, and turning to Helena he added, in a respectful tone:

"Will you endeavor to walk, my lady? We will support you."

Seeing the Turk, she turned away her head with a frightened expression, exclaiming:

"Go away from me! Morosini, save me from these monsters!"

"Fear not, Helena," replied the Italian, "I am with you. This man will do you no harm. Let us try to raise you."

Reassured by these words, she offered no further resistance, and the two men gently raised the lady to her feet. Though weak, she was able to stand, and leaning on Morosini, she walked onward, preceded by the Turk. They directed their steps towards the nearest house, before which stood a follower of Mahomet. A few words were exchanged between both Turks, and the stranger who accompanied Morosini and Helena bade them enter, saying:

"Here you will be safe."

The house seemed abandoned and, within it, all was confusion. It appeared evident that it had been given given over to pillage. Broken furniture lay scattered in all directions, but every object of value had disappeared. Helena was conducted to one of the sleeping apartments and laid upon a couch.

"You need fear nothing, lady," spoke the Turk, "you are here under my protection."

"Where is Dimitrios?" she asked with anxiety.

"Helena, you need rest; Dimitrios is safe, calm your fears," answered Morosini.

"Oh, they are hiding the worst from me!" cried the poor girl, mid tears and sobs, "Dimitrios is dead, or he would be here."

Morosini endeavored, as much as possible, to hide the fears which tormented him, but, in spite of his efforts, his countenance betrayed him.

"Vincent," said Helena, "I see that you have nothing reassuring to tell me. You know not where my brother is. Tell me the truth."

"Helena, must you not confide in God? Rest assured that your brother will come to you."

The Turk gazed in silence upon the suffering girl; finally, he spoke:

"I will go in quest of your brother, and will bring him back to you."

"But you do not know my brother."

"I know him. I saw him when he was a prisoner among us. I am a friend, trust me."

Morosini turned an enquiring glance upon him, saying:

"Are you the friend of whom Dimitrios spoke; are you Selim?"

"I am not Selim, but I am Selim's friend; you shall hear more later. Meanwhile, remain with the lady. I will place a strong guard at the door; you will have naught to fear."

With these words the Turk departed.

CHAPTER XXI.

What was happening in St. Sophia? The abomination of desolation was in the holy place. For centuries it had been a Christian temple in which the name of Christ had been daily pronounced with reverence, and the sacrifice of the New Law had been offered upon its altars by a Christian priesthood, though for a long time that priesthood had been separated from the great body of the Christian Church. Henceforward, the name of the prophet of Mecca was to take the place of that of the Redeemer. Around the sacred edifice stood a crowd of wailing captives who had sought refuge in the church. They were being divided among the Mussulman conquerors. The male captives were bound with cords, the females with their veils and girdles. Senators and slaves were linked together, prelates were bound to those of inferior dignity, plebeian youths to noble maids. In this general captivity, the ranks of society were confounded. Children had been torn from their parents, husbands from their wives, and the hardhearted soldier heeded not the lamentations of his victims. The loud wailings of consecrated virgins who had been torn from the altar, arose above the universal cries of grief, while mothers detested their fecundity and deplored the fate of their infants.

It was while this dismal spectacle was witnessed at the doors of St. Sophia, that the youthful conqueror rode up to the eastern entrance of the temple. Upon the face of Mahomet lay an expression of pity, and even of sympathy for his captives. He gazed upon the multitude with compassion, and, as he approached the entrance to the church, he was heard to exclaim:

"I will be the friend and father of these unfortunates."

The Sultan rode in at the eastern door. As he entered the edifice, followed by a multitude, a mollah, at his bidding, ascended the pulpit whence the voice of the Christian preacher had so frequently been heard, and, under the lofty dome of St. Sophia, resounded for the first time the cry:

"God is great, and Mahomet is his prophet."

Beneath the pulpit stood two men. Joy was plainly pictured upon their countenances. The eyes of one were riveted upon the Sultan. He is no stranger to you, reader, you have seen him ere this; it is Nicolaus Lecapenos. When the Sultan left the church that had now become a mosque, the two men followed at a respectful distance. The work of spoliation began. The dome of St. Sophia was stripped of its ornaments, precious objects of gold and silver and the sacred vessels fell into the hands of the sacriligious invaders; nothing was spared.

No sooner had Nicolaus and his companion reached the Hippodrome than they were brought face to face with the Turk who, a short time before, had left Helena and Morosini, to go in quest of Dimitrios. Surprise pictured itself both on the face of the Greek and on that of the Turk. There was a mutual recognition. The countenance of the former bore evidence of unrestrained satisfaction, while that of the latter showed signs of the disgust which filled his heart and which he endeavored to conceal.

Nicolaus recognizing Fortuny, in spite of his change of costume, exclaimed: "Fortuny, I had thought thee dead! Hast thou joined the faithful?"

"You understand," replied the Catalan, "that the reason why I did not return to you arose from the fact that, during the siege, I could find no opportunity of entering the city."

"Well, at all events," spoke Nicolaus, "I am delighted to see you. I have had numberless hair-breadth escapes. The Emperor did all he could to find me, under pretence of exchanging me for Dimitrios, but I was equal to the ruse. It is not such an easy task to ensnare this fox. But now—ha, ha!—I am free, free as the birds of the air; I replenish my lungs again with the pure air of heaven, the beautiful sun shines upon me, Constantinople is ours; there is only one thing wanting to my happiness, and that is, you know it, the possession of Irene. But the Sultan has promised her to me, and no one shall thwart me, I assure you."

"Speak not too soon, friend," replied Fortuny.

"What do you mean?" asked Nicolaus with surprise.

"Did you not send me to Thessalonica?"

"I did."

"I have been there."

"And how is Irene?"

"That is more than I can tell."

"Speak, man, what do you mean?"

"I mean that the bird has flown."

"Impossible."

It is not only not impossible, but it is true. I found no trace of Irene, her father, nor the guard."

"Fortuny, you are deceiving me."

"As sure as the sun is shining upon us, so sure it is that I am telling you the truth."

"I will go to Thessalonica myself; I will find them, as truly as my name is Nicolaus."

"You may do as you like. When will you start?"

"This very night. But, tell me, where is Dimitrios?"

"How can you ask that question? Do you not know that nearly all the men who were fighting have fallen, and that all those who were taken under arms have been put to death by the Sultan's orders? The Emperor himself has disappeared, although Mohammed has ordered that search should be made for him. Dimitrios, no doubt, lies among the slain."

There was a smile upon the lips of Nicolaus, as he replied:

"So much the better; my rival is out of the way. Although I feel kindly towards him on account of his interest in me, I would rather see him dead than alive, on account of Irene."

A look of aversion passed over the face of Fortuny.

"Where is my reward?" he asked.

"It was only promised on condition that you brought me news of Irene"

"Is it thus you make bargains, Greek? We shall meet again, Lecapenos."

Fortuny turned upon his heels, and, ere Nicolaus had time to recall him, he was gone. On reaching the Mese, he saw a Turk standing with two saddled horses beside him. Holding out a piece of gold, he said:

"Give me one of those animals."

The Mahometan's eyes fell greedily upon the glittering metal, and, without hesitation, he made the exchange. In an instant Fortuny sprang into the saddle and galloped off toward the walls. Passing through the gate Phenar which was wide open, he proceeded in the direction of the camp. * * * * *

Meanwhile, Selim sat in his tent. Beside him lay upon an improvised couch Dimitrios, pale and wan. His head was tied with a bandage.

"Dimitrios," spoke the priest, "has not Providence been kind to you? After saving the life of your soul, God has also saved the life of your body. Had I not been among the Turks who rushed first into the city, I would not have seen you fall. Your escape has been miraculous. When I saw the scimitar descend upon your head, I gave you up for lost. I was too late to avert the blow. Thank Heaven! your wound is not serious. Your angel must have held his shield above you, for a blow like the one you received must have killed you. It broke your helmet. As soon as you fell, I rushed to your side. It was impossible to carry you to the right or to the left, for the multitude, storming into the city, pressed on all sides, hence I dragged you along for a considerable distance, until I found a free space."

"Father," answered the youth, in a feeble voice, "you have saved my life; I owe you more than I can ever repay, but would it not have been better if I had died? Alas! life, bereft of all, is worse than death. Constantine has fallen, Morosini is no more, Helena is, perhaps, dead, and Irene is lost to me forever. Why must I survive them? I alone to weep over the ashes of the dead! Why did I not fall with thee, Paleologos, with thee, my bosom friend, Morosini? Then would I now be with Helena in a better world, and from beyond the skies my prayers would protect Irene."

Selim gazed, with tears in his eyes, upon the face of the youthful sufferer.

"Speak not thus, Dimitrios, I beseech you," he said, "your imagination renders things worse than they are. Before we returned to the camp, I searched the spot where you told me Morosini had stood; there was no trace of his body. I do not believe he is killed. I have sent Fortuny in quest of Helena, be sure that he will move Heaven and earth to find her. He was in advance of me when my eye first fell upon you whom he did not notice. I remember distinctly that, at the moment when I flew to your side, I caught a glimpse of him rushing on in the front rank. He has surely reached the city in safety, and, perhaps, even now is on his way back with the good news that Helena is safe. One thing I must require of you; that is strict secrecy in regard to your identity. Not a soul must know you. You must pass for my slave; I will disguise you in such a manner that even Helena would not recognize you. Be cheerful, and hope for the best."

"Welcome, Hassan!" cried a voice outside of the tent.

Dimitrios started, while Selim jumped to his feet and ran to the entrance. Fortuny stood there in conversation with a man. Selim went out to him and drew him aside.

"Well, Fortuny, what news?"

"Ah, Padre, good news, good news! Let me go into your tent first and quench my thirst, I am dying for some juice of the grape."

"No, Fortuny, wait a moment, we have no time to

lose. Dimitrios is there, but he is prostrated and any sudden intelligence of a startling nature might prove injurious to him."

"Dimitrios there! O, this is too good! Now Helena will rejoice!"

"Helena lives, Fortuny?"

"She lives, my father, and she is safe."

Selim raised his eyes to Heaven and breathed a silent prayer of thanksgiving, then added the inquiry:

"And Morosini?"

"He, too, is safe and with Helena."

Fortuny related the events of the day, taking especial care not to omit his accidental meeting with Nicolaus.

"So!" said Selim, "he is going to Thessalonica! We have, then, no time to lose. Saddle the three fleetest horses that you can find, bring them here within half an hour."

Selim entered the tent. Dimitrios raised himself on his elbow and gazed eagerly at the priest.

"Did I not tell you to be of good cheer, Dimitrios?

"Speak, father, relieve my suspense, what news have you?"

"Excellent news, my boy."

"Is Helena alive?"

"Yes, my son, alive and safe."

"Thank God! Have you heard of Morosini?"

"Morosini is with Helena."

"Oh, the faithful friend! Father, let us go to them."

"We shall go to them within an hour. Think you that you are strong enough?"

"Oh, yes! I feel a new strength within me, my life returns, my blood flows more freely."

"Await my return, dear boy."

Selim left the tent and in a short time returned with a garment under his arm. It was a short tunic and girdle. Dimitrios, who had been already divested of his armor, put on the tunic.

"Now," said Selim, "you will have to make a sacrifice, you must allow me to cut off those locks."

"I am at your disposal, father."

"In an instant, the beautiful hair of Dimitrios lay upon the ground. Selim now opened several boxes containing ointments and cosmetics; a few strokes of a camel's hair brush over the face of the youth produced a marvellous transformation. He was no longer the handsome young soldier, but a withered man, apparently about fifty years of age. Selim's words had been true, not even Helena could have known him. The preparations had hardly been completed, than Fortuny entered. Walking towards Dimitrios and extending his hand, he said:

"I suppose you remember me. Your escape from the Turkish camp would have been impossible had I not fallen on purpose. I wanted you to escape."

Dimitrios smiled in reply. The two men assisted the youth to his feet and helped him to mount his horse. Placing themselves on either side of him, they rode on toward the city.

CHAPTER XXII.

The day, the most terrible one in the history of the Byzantine Empire, the day of its death, the 29th of May, 1453, was about to be numbered with countless other days which lie buried in the grave of the past. The hours had dragged along slowly over the heart of poor Helena, as she anxiously awaited tidings of her brother. As time passed, and the Turk returned not, hope began to desert her, in spite of the cheering words of Morosini. Nourishment was brought to her by one of the guards Fortuny had stationed at the house, but she refused to touch food, while tears unceasingly coursed down her cheeks. The sun had set, and the shades of twilight gradually settled over the earth; still there was no news of Dimitrios.

"Oh, Morosini!" moaned the heart-broken girl; "my brother will never return!"

"Do not lose courage so easily, Helena," answered her friend.

"Have I not waited an entire day? If Dimitrios is not dead, he is, at least, a prisoner."

"That does not follow. May he not be searching for us?"

A heavy step was heard, and suddenly the door was pushed open. A Turk entered, but it was not the one whom they expected. Both Helena and Vincent gazed at him in mute surprise.

"Fear not," the stranger said, "I am Selim, the friend of Dimitrios."

"Welcome, thrice welcome!" exclaimed Morosini.

"Where is my brother?" cried Helena.

"Your brother lives, lady."

"He lives! I thank Thee, Oh, God of Mercy! My brother lives? Where is he, why does he not come to me?"

"He will come, but I desired to prepare you. Your brother is disguised; it is necessary for his safety; you will not recognize him."

"Oh, bring him to me, let me see him!"

"Your desire shall be accomplished, I go to fetch him."

Selim went out and, in ess than a minute, returned with Dimitrios. Morosin gazed in astonishment. He would not have known his friend.

"Is this Dimitrios?" he exclaimed.

"Oh, my brother," cried Helena, "God has brought us back from the tomb!"

"We can never sufficiently thank Him," replied the youth, embracing his sister, then, turning to Morosini, he added:

"Vincent, my friend, thy fidelity binds thee to me with ties that not even death can break."

Morosini grasped the hand of his friend in silence.

"My friends," said Selim, "we have no time to lose, prepare to leave Constantinople this very night. I have sent a faaithful servant to engage a vessel. Morosini, you must submit to a disguise, for otherwise your life will be in danger, and the Lady Helena must wear her veil the entire length of the journey. I know that Greek ladies are always veiled in public, but I simply remind her, lest, in an unguarded moment, she might inadvertently neglect this custom."

"We place ourselves into your hands, command us in all things," said Dimitrios.

Selim now proceeded to use his paint on Morosini, until the young man was no longer recognizable. Within an hour, Fortuny returned with the information that he had engaged a Turkish vessel to convey the party to Thessalonica. Very little time was spent in preparation, for they had nothing to take with them, save the clothes they wore. The house of Dimitrios had been pillaged, together with the rest of the city, and he had, consequently, lost his property. Morosini, it is true, was still wealthy, but his wealth lay in a distant country. Fortuny, however, and Selim, commanded both influence and money, and, herewith, they had induced the Turkish captain to take them to Salonica. Selim himself had procured leave of absence from the army for an indefinite period.

Dark night lay over Constantinople when the little party boarded the vessel that was to bear them away forever, and Dimitrios and Helena bade their native city a last farewell. It was a solemn moment. While Dimitrios leaned over the side of the vessel, as she slowly moved out of the harbor, and the buildings of Constantinople stood faintly outlined against the shadows of the night, the past, with all its bliss forever gone, and with all its horrors, rushed to his memory, like the sudden flash of recollection that shall burst upon every child of Adam, when time shall be no more. He seemed to live again, as he lived in the "long ago," mid the untainted joys of childhood's blessed period. That noble father and that gentle mother, whose loving voices still sounded in his ears out of the distance of an unforgotten past, were sleeping the sleep of the dead, beneath the soil now desecrated by the ruthless invader who respects not the symbol of Redemption that casts its shadow over the tomb where Christians lie. Mid the sorrows conjured before the living by the voice of the dead, there arose, too, a vision of beauty and innocence, a vision, alas! that had faded.

"Irene, Irene," thought Dimitrios, "how pleasantly the hours sped away in thy company! Oh, how sadly I remember the last glance I cast upon thy fair form as it vanished before my eyes in the house of thy father, on that fatal evening that sent me forth an exile from a spot I loved so well!"

From the innermost depths of his soul, there sounded a voice as he heard it on that very same evening:

"There is nothing true but Heaven."

The young man raised his eyes. The stars were shedding their soft radiance upon the turbulent scenes of death and desolation, over which the night had cast its mantle. They looked down upon the exiled son of Byzantium, and, as his eyes fell upon the dark waters of the Golden Horn, he saw the wavering reflection of those stars beneath the moving waves.

"An image," thought he, "of time and eternity. There, all is steadfast and lasting, even more so than the firmament, which stands while kingdoms and empires crumble into dust; here, there is an ever moving, ever changing variety and vicissitude, like the unstable reflections brneath us."

Recollections of the past few days crowded upon him. He still felt the warm grasp of the Emperor's hand, that hand now stiffened in death, he still heard the echo of that voice, a voice now hushed forever. It seemed to sound out of the silence of the grave: "My children, farewell!"

"How, then, has the mighty fallen! Oh, Constantine, I shall never again behold thee! But thou art happy in thy sleep. Slumber, then, hero, and rest from thy labors until the day when the grave shall surrender its dead." Emotions like these filled his soul which, from scenes of woe and carnage, was turning to a last relic of happy days, his sister Helena, when a hand was laid upon his shoulders, and a voice sounded in his ears:

"Dimitrios, why stand you here, thus pensive? Do you not know that excessive sorrow unnerves the soul? Rather prepare yourself for the labors that await you."

Dimitrios, turning, beheld Selim.

"Thanks, my father, my mind had wandered off into the past."

The priest now led Dimitrios to Helena and Morosini, and some time was spent in conversation, in which Selim endeavored to raise the drooping spirits of the afflicted Greeks.

The night passed, and a sleepless one it was for the travelers. When morning dawned, the first light of day revealed a vessel in the distance, sailing in the same direction."

"Do you see that craft?" said Fortuny, "I know it, it sailed a few hours before we did. It carries Nicolaus Lecapenos."

"The wretch has been quicker than we were, but we have right on our side," replied Selim.

At this moment a Turk advanced towards the two men.

"They have found the Emperor," he spoke, "I learned this just before leaving the city."

"Is the Emperor alive?" inquired Fortuny, surprised.

"No. I mean they have found his body. The first thing the Sultan did on entering the city was to order a search for the sovereign of Byzantium. The body was finally discovered, but it was so disfigured that it could only be identified by the golden eagles on the mail shoes. The Sultan had the head struck off and he has ordered that it should be sent around to the chief cities."

Both Selim and Fortuny turned away their heads with tokens of evident disgust.

On board the other ship, which was several miles in advance of the one which carried Dimitrios and his companions, a strange spectacle was seen. On the deck of the vessel lay huddled together a number of unfortunate Greeks, who were being carried away from their homes to be dispersed in various sections of the Ottoman Empire and languish in slavery. They were, nearly all, young persons of both sexes. Bound by huge chains of iron, they sat with drooping heads and closed eyes, as if indifferent to their fate; the mark of despair was upon their countenances. At the stern of the ship two men were engaged in earnest conversation. They were both clad in Turkish costume, but the countenance of one showed that he was a Greek. Observe them attentively and you will recognize the one as Nicolaus Lecapenos, the other as Ali, the Turk, from whom Helena was rescued by Morosini.

"You may rely upon my words, Nicolaus," spoke the latter, "I know where they are, I will conduct you to them. I want no reward, nothing, nothing but revenge. He made me a laughing stock, he despised me openly, he shall pay for it, I will have revenge. Ah! little does he dream that I know all."

"Are you perfectly sure, Ali, that Ismael has Irene in his power?"

"As sure as you are a living man, and that, too, by the orders of the Sultan. Mohammed has simply used you as a tool and he would care no more about cutting off your head, than he would about killing a fly. He has heard of the wonderful beauty of the Greek maiden and he has determined to enrich his harem with the golden sunshine of her presence. Ismael is merely the custodian of the girl. Her father and brother are left her for the present, that she may be more reconciled to her fate, but, in a short time, you may be sure of it, they will be removed."

"If what you say is true, as I have no doubt it is, how can I compete with the Sultan? It would be madness to attempt it."

"If you follow my directions, you will succeed. At the time we appoint, you will have a boat hidden among the rushes not far from the castle. I will gain admittance as a workman, for the place is undergoing repairs. No one there knows me, for Ismael will be absent for several weeks. I am well acquainted with the place, in which there is a subterranean passage. I will endeavor to persuade the girl that I am her deliverer; if she consents, so much the better; if she resists, she will be drugged. I will save her father and brother if I can; if not, they must be left to their fate."

"The expedition is a hazardous one."

"It is; but if managed prudently, it will succeed. Forget not that I will have confederates; there are enough dare-devils in this world who are willing to risk their lives for a few gold pieces. And think of the reward: you will have Irene, and I, revenge. When Mohammed hears that his prey has escaped, he will be furious and my enemy's head will fall. Oh, it is glorious to think of it! Ismael, Ismael, thou wilt never insult Ali again!"

"Give me your hand, Ali, the affair is settled."

Absorbed in conversation, Nicolaus had not noticed an old woman seated at some distance from them. She was near enough to overhear their words, but she seemed to heed them not. Her chin rested in her hands, while her elbows were supported by her knees. An attentive observer would have noticed that her eyes would occasionally steal a furtive glance at the speakers. The woman was evidently not a captive, and she had, probably, paid for her passage.

The ship on which Nicolaus sailed arrived at Thessalonica several hours before the one that carried Dimitrios. No sooner had Lecapenos set foot on land than he directed his steps towards the house where Irene had been detained. He found that he had been correctly informed by Fortuny. The mansion was deserted. He left the spot, determined to execute his plans, not noticing that, at some distance behind him, walked the old crone, bent under the weight of years, whom we saw on board the ship.

CHAPTER XXIII.

Two weeks had passed since the arrival of Dimitrios at Thessalonica. All inquiries concerning Irene had proved fruitless, no one knew whither she had gone. A heavy load weighed upon the soul of Dimitrios, and clouds of anguish gathered over him. The efforts of Selim to console him were in vain; even Helena could hardly elicit a faint smile. Still, there was that in his countenance that denoted a fixed purpose and a firm determination. Wherever there seemed a possibility of obtaining information, Selim sought for it. He was standing outside of the door of the house in which he had placed his wards, when his attention was drawn to a Greek with tattered garments, who, at that moment, was passing. The man seemed shy, and he glanced from side to side, with a frightened expression upon his face.

"I greet thee, stranger," said Selim.

The man stood still, but replied not.

"You have nothing to fear. I see that you are a Greek. I am a friend of the Greeks. Perhaps you may have fled from Constantinople; if so, you are weary and, perhaps, need refreshment; will you accept my hospitality today?"

The stranger, raising his eyes to Heaven, exclaimed with the words of the Liturgy:

"Kyrie eleison, Lord, have mercy on us!"

"You have been witness of awful scenes, no doubt, my friend; my house, humble as it is, is yours."

"Thanks, kind-hearted man," replied the stranger timidly, "I will rest awhile beneath thy roof."

Selim led the way and the Greek followed him into the small house, which had been engaged for the party during their stay in Thessalonica. Dimitrios and Morosini sat facing each other in silence, Helena was in the apartment set aside for her use.

"Dimitrios," said Selim, "here is an unfortunate countryman of yours who has fled from the Turks."

The stranger looked more at ease when he heard the words, but he gazed with surprise from Morosini to Dimitrios, neither of whom he would have taken for a Christian. Selim, noticing his embarassment, said:

"We are clad as Turks, in order to escape observation. Be seated, and tell us of the unfortunate city."

The Greek began thus:

"Words are unequal to the task. Tongue cannot express, mind cannot conceive the abomination of desolation that these eyes have beheld. I have seen the bodies of the slain heaped up in the public places. More than two thousand have fallen by the sword. Sixty thousand of our unhappy countrymen have been carried off to the fleet and the camp, to be dispersed among Mohametan nations. The Sultan, on his arrival in the city, seemed touched by the sight that met his eyes. He declared that he would be the protector of our people. It was lying deceit and hypocrisy. But how could we help being deceived? The Sultan ransomed several persons of rank, to others he gave their liberty. Many, deluded by his words, cast themselves upon his protection, alas! to become his victims. I was among the number of those who implored his clemency, and only my flight has saved me. The Sultan has left the city, but before doing so, he gave orders that the noblest of his captives should be beheaded in cold blood. They have fallen, the sons of Byzantium, fallen under the deadly swords of the infidel. Numbers of our poor people are scattered over the country, flying from death and disgrace. I have seen them driven like herds of cattle through the streets of the city, their trembling pace being quickened by menaces and blows; but, alas! the end is not yet. Shall I proceed? My tongue almost refuses to perform its service in relating such horrors."

"Yes, go on," cried Dimitrios, "tell us all."

"Well, a young lady of our nation was made a slave by one of the pashas. She was of noble birth and of surpassing beauty and hardly seventeen years of age."

Dimitrios looked on with suppressed anxiety, his eyes riveted on the speaker, while his countenance assumed an ashen hue. The stranger proceeded:

"As I said, her beauty was unsurpassed; the Orient had never witnessed anything so charming. The pasha deemed her a present worthy of the Sultan. Mahomet accepted the gift and became entirely subdued by the charms of the poor girl. To this new passion he yielded himself entirely. It diverted his attention from his duties, and, for several days, he refused to see his ministers and the principal officers of the army. The men murmured, both officers and soldiers complained, but none dared remonstrate with him, so terrible is his wrath. Finally, one of his most faithful officers, Mustapha Pasha, informed him of the discourses which the Janissaries were holding against him. The Sultan remained silent, as if considering what course to pursue.

Finally he ordered Mustapha to summon, the next day, all the pashas, the guards and the troops for a review. To Irene he paid the most devoted attention, more than ever."

"Great Heavens!" cried Dimitrios, "no, it cannot be Irene! impossible."

"What ails thee, friend?" asked the stranger; "perhaps I have been imprudent."

"Go on," exclaimed Dimitrios, "let me hear the rest, tell me all."

"I fear to continue."

"I beseech you, proceed; it was only an exclamation drawn forth by the similarity of the name with one I know; proceed, I pray."

"I said, that to the lady he began to pay greater attentions than ever, giving her numerous proofs of his love. On the morrow he bade her maids exert all their care and skill in dressing her. Taking her by the hand, he led her into the middle of the assembled troops, when, tearing off her veil, he haughtily asked the pachas if they had ever seen a more perfect beauty. All the officers praised her to the skies and congratulated the Sultan. Thereupon, Mohammed took hold of the hair of the beautiful Greek and, with the other hand he drew his sword, at one stroke, separating her head from her body, while he exclaimed: *"This sword, whenever I please, can cut asunder the ties of love."*

Selim sprang to his feet, as if touched by an electric spark, Morosini clenched his fist, and Dimitrios, poor Dimitrios! his hands fell lifeless by his side, his eyes closed, his head sank upon his breast, his body leaned to one side, he fell heavily upon the floor.

"Great God! what have I done?" exclaimed the stranger.

In an instant Selim and Morosini were by the side of the prostrate man; they laid him upon a couch and applied various remedies to recall him to consciousness.

For a long time Dimitrios lay deprived of his senses. Helena was nearly distracted with grief, while his friends did all in their power to revive him. While they were thus engaged, Fortuny entered. On learning the cause of the illness of Dimitrios, he exclaimed:

"How unfortunate! Why was I not here?"

He then proceeded to inform them that the alarm of Dimitrios was utterly without foundation, that he had learned the same sad history from another source and that, finally, the victim of the cruelty of Mahomet was not Irene Diogenes, but another noble lady of the same name.

After long and patient labor on the part of his friends, Dimitrios gradually returned to his senses, though it was some time before he recollected where he was and could connect the present with the past.

"My dear boy," said Selim, "how foolish you have been!"

"Oh, Father! the blow was terrible."

"But, my son, there was no blow at all, except that inflicted upon our common sentiment of humanity."

"But is not Irene—?"

"Yes, but not your Irene."

"Father, are you certain?"

"Perfectly sure, my son."

"How do you know?"

"Fortuny has it from a reliable source."

"You are not deceiving me, Father?"

"You do not think me capable of such an act?"

"Oh, no! forgive me, I am much calmer now."

A loud knock was heard upon the outer door. We must not forget to state, ere we proceed, that the Greek who had related the tragic end of the unfortunate Grecian lady had, after partaking of refreshment, proceeded on his way. Hearing the rapping at the door, Fortuny proceeded to open a small aperture, which allowed him to see who was outside, while he remained unseen. There stood an old woman, stooping under the weight of years. Over her head she wore a coarse veil, which almost completely covered it, exposing to view only her eyes. She is the same creature whom we beheld on board the vessel where sat Nicolaus Lecapenos.

"Who art thou?" inquired, Fortuny.

"A harmless old woman."

"What dost thou want?"

"I would see Selim."

"What hast thou to communicate?"

"A matter of the gravest importance," and she added in a lower tone, "regarding Irene Diogenes."

Fortuny, bidding her wait, returned to communicate in a whisper this intelligence to Selim. The eye of of the priest brightened.

"Dimitrios," said he, turning to the young Greek, "an urgent affair requires my attention; converse with Helena until my return. Morosini, and you, Fortuny, accompany me."

The heart of Dimitrios beat violently, but, without showing his emotion, he nodded acquiescence. Fortuny now proceeded to unfasten the door and admit the strange visitor into an inner room, where Selim and

Morosini awaited her. She bowed profoundly, as she entered, and accepted a seat offered her by the Italian.

"My good woman," spoke Selim, "what have you to communicate to me?"

She looked around anxiously.

"Fear nothing," he added, "you may trust my friends as you trust me, and no one can overhear us."

"I know where Irene is," she began, in a voice that sounded strangely melodious for a woman of her age.

"Speak," replied Selim, "speak, good woman, give us all information, no reward will be too great for you."

"I wish for no reward, save the testimony of my conscience."

"What, then, do you know?"

"Diogenes and his family remained for some time in this city, and they were removed no one knew whither; but I have discovered all. The removal took place by the Sultan's orders. He had learned of the extraordinary beauty of Irene, and he determined to possess her himself. In consequence of this he decided that, together with her father and brother, she should be detained at the castle of Sestos on the Hellespont."

"Sestos!" exclaimed Morosini, "the spot where Solyman crossed the Hellespont some years ago?"

"The same," answered the old woman.

"Go on," said Selim.

"I have now told you where Irene is. You understand what her fate will be, if she is left there. She must be rescued."

"If it costs us every drop of blood," exclaimed Morosini.

"Be not impetuous, young man," replied the stranger,

"let prudence hold the helm. Will you listen to my suggestion?"

"Proceed," replied Selim.

"An attempt will be made to rescue her by those into whose hands she should not fall."

Here she related what she knew of the plans of Nicolaus and Ali, and added:

"Thus far, they have not been able to execute their design, because Ismael had unexpectedly arrived at the castle. However, he has again left it, and it is rumored that he will soon return with the Sultan himself. Thus, you see, there is no time to be lost. This is what I propose: There is a small vessel lying here at anchor. I know the captain. He is a Moor from the south of Spain and a friend of the Christians, but he hates the Turks. I have spoken with him and he has agreed to take your party on board for a compensation. He has with him an amount of armor and weapons, and he will be of service to you, for he is a daring man. Let your party board his vessel to-night. I will accompany you to guide your movements. Nicolaus and his companions have already started by the overland route. The time set aside for the execution of their plans is the night of the 20th of this month, June, at midnight, only three days from now. We will arrange matters thus, that we arrive on the spot at dusk, and land after dark. We will then hide ourselves opposite the subterranean passage, through which Irene will be brought—the very passage through which Prince Solyman entered the castle. Nicolaus is far from suspecting that his secret is known. As soon as I whistle, you will know that Ali is leaving the castle with Irene. You will then divide your party, the half will render

Nicolaus and his companions harmless, while the other half will overpower Ali and rescue Irene. The rest we must leave to Providence. If we gain the vessel in safety, we will immediately set all sail for the Island of Rhodes."

"My good woman," said Selim, "your story is, indeed, marvellous, but what proofs can you give us that the facts are as you state?"

"Proofs? None. I have only my word to offer, the word of a stranger; but remember that a drowning man catches at a straw; you would find Irene at any cost, you know that she is not in Thessalonica, I assure you that I speak the truth; if you pay no heed to my advice, you may lose your only chance of finding her, and think of the terrible consequences if she is not found."

"Well, good woman," answered Selim, "it is a matter of life and death, we will catch at the straw and risk it. To-night we will be on board the vessel, to which you will conduct us,"

"Well said," replied the old woman, "you shall find me faithful. At midnight, when Thessalonica is plunged in sleep, I will meet you here."

She arose and departed.

CHAPTER XXIV.

The hot sun of a glowing summer day in June bathed the landscape in a flood of light. The waters of the Hellespont lay calm and lifeless at the foot of the castle of Sestos, reflecting upon their heated bosom the brilliant rays of the noon-day, and stretching on one side towards the Propontis, on the other, toward the Ægean Sea. Nearly directly south from Sestos, on the opposite shores of the straits, lay the town of Abydos. All nature seemed sweltering in the heat, plants were drooping, while animals instinctively sought the shade. In a room of the castle, overlooking the Hellespont, sat Irene, pale and worn. Her eyes were sunken, her cheeks, bloodless, but there still shone around her the reflection of her extraordinary beauty. Opposite her stood John Diogenes. His grey locks hung carelessly on his shoulders, and his wasted frame showed the agony through which he had passed. Basil reclined on a couch near by.

"My child," spoke Diogenes, "if we are left as we are now, I feel contented, but when we awaken in the morning, we know not what the day will bring forth."

"Father," replied the girl, "we are in the hands of One more powerful than the Sultan; without His permission not a hair of our head will suffer."

There was a rap at the door, and the maid of Irene entered, bowing profoundly before her mistress. Pointing towards the door, she pronounced the words:

"Ismael Pasha."

Irene turned and beheld a tall Turk of rather handsome countenance, the same whom we saw at Constantinople together with Ali. Her face grew pale, her frame trembled. John Diogenes clenched his fist. Advancing toward the lady, Ismael prostrated himself before her, as though she were his sovereign.

"Hail, Sultana!" he exclaimed in Greek, "my master sends thee greeting."

Irene answered not. Ismael arose, and, standing respectfully before her, again spoke:

"Sultana, my master greets thee."

"Why thus address me? I am not a Sultana," answered Irene.

"You are Sultana, noble lady. My master has chosen you for his bride. He who wields the sceptre over the East and the West, will share his power with you."

"Beseech your master, in my name, to choose another, I am but a lowly Grecian maiden, unfit to reign over an empire."

"Mohammed will have no other, the light of your eyes shines within his soul."

"Spare your pains," said Diogenes, "my daughter cannot accept the offer of the Sultan."

Ismael cast a threatening look upon him. Diogenes was silent for the sake of prudence.

"What answer shall I bring to our sovereign lord?" the Turk asked of Irene.

"Tell him that I am a Christian."

"He knows this, but he will allow you the free exercise of your religion. Moreover, think of the glory in store for you: you shall be seated on the throne of Constantinople, all that your heart can desire will be yours. My master is young and powerful, he will render you happy."

"Your master already has a Sultana."

"He will make you the first in the realm."

"It would be unjust."

"My master's will is justice."

"But my religion forbids me to marry a man who is already wedded."

"My master has as many spouses as he wishes."

"This gives me no right to become his spouse."

"Think well, lady, before you reject the flattering offer of the Sultan. You belong to Mohammed."

"I belong to God."

"Your God will not deliver you from his hands."

"I am betrothed."

"No one shall come between you and the Sultan. Remember that you are in his power, you shall become his bride, or a dweller in his harem. I advise you to choose the former. Once more, what answer shall I bring to my master?"

"Tell him that I thank him for the honor that he offers me, but that my conscience forbids me to accept."

"Foolish girl!" cried Ismael, in wrath, "thousands would kiss the feet of the Sultan in gratitude for an honor you reject, but it matters not, the Sultan himself will visit you."

Ismael retired.

"My poor child," cried Diogenes, "we are in a sad plight, what shall we do? I see no hope."

"Confide, father, remember Joseph in the prison of Egypt, Daniel in the lion's den, the three children in the fiery furnace. The same God who protected them, can protect us."

"But He seems to have abandoned us."

"He never forsakes those who confide in Him; there may be rescue at the eleventh hour."

"The hope seems vain. Constantinople has fallen, the Emperor is dead, all the young men have been killed, whence can rescue come? We have no right to expect a miracle."

"And yet I hope against hope."

"My child, this is foolish. Be not angry with your father, but allow him to make his thoughts known to you."

"Speak, father, speak."

"You know, dearest, what a fate will be ours, if you continue to resist the Sultan. His wrath is terrible. There is a way of reconciling the acceptance of his offer with your conscience."

The girl looked at her father in amazement.

"Father," she said, "I understand you not."

"Of course, the Sultan can be the lawful husband of only one woman, but we do not know with certainty, that anyone of the inmates of the harem is his lawful wife. If we find out that the Sultan is married, you know that the Greek church permits divorce in case of the infidelity of one of the parties. Should you find that the Sultan is free to marry, may not the dire sorrows that surround us be a sufficient excuse for your accepting his offer?"

"Father, father, I am surprised. Would you see your daughter the wife of a Mussulman?"

"My child, marriage with an infidel is allowed in a case like this."

"No, father, never! Moreover, what would Dimitrios say?"

"If Dimitrios is still alive, he may be married by this time. How can you think of one who has been thus unfaithful to you?"

"Dimitrios unfaithful! No, I will not, cannot believe it. Rather would I believe that Mount Pindus should move itself and float upon the waters of the Propontis, than that Dimitrios is unfaithful."

"My child, will you then condemn yourself, your father, your brother, Basil, to a cruel death?"

"My dearest father, I love you more than tongue can express, my heart bleeds for Basil; but, oh, death, yes death a thousand times, rather than dishonor!"

"There will be no dishonor, if you become the lawful wife of the Sultan."

"But if I cannot become the wife of the Sultan?"

"In that case we must die together."

"How can I be unfaithful to Dimitrios?"

"Dimitrios is not your husband; you were engaged to him, and if that engagement had not been dissolved by his meanness, there would now be sufficient reason to dissolve it."

"Oh, father! tempt me not, my heart is breaking. Let me rest now, we will converse on this subject again."

"My poor child, forgive me if I have pained you. I will summon your maid, she will conduct you to your room."

"No, father, thank you. I would prefer to be alone."

Irene kissed her father and arose to leave the room. Basil, who, thus far, had listened in silence, now rushed toward her. He cast himself upon his knees before her and, extending his hands imploringly, exclaimed:

"Irene, be not hard-hearted, let your heart be touched. Yield to the entreaties of father, let not our blood be shed; save him, Irene, save me, save yourself. Turn not a deaf ear to my prayers."

"What can I do, Basil, my poor brother?"

"Say yes to the Sultan, be his wife; do, Irene, save us."

"But, my brother, if it offends God?"

"It does not offend God, He could not be so cruel."

"Basil, ask me no longer, let me rest now."

Irene fled from the room. When she arrived in her own apartment, she cast herself upon her knees. With eyes raised to Heaven, and the hot tears streaming down her face, she prayed:

"O God! it is for Thee I am suffering. Help me in this hour of peril, turn not away Thy ears from the supplications of Thy handmaid, give not Thy inheritance to the beasts of prey. Touch the heart of my father, let him not become a tempter."

A sweet peace fell upon the soul of the afflicted girl, terror had vanished, for, though walking midst the shadows of death, she feared not evil, God was with her. Gradually her eyelids drooped, her head fell forward, she sank slowly upon the ground, exhausted nature succumbed and a deep slumber lulled the emotions of her afflicted soul to rest. The hours passed unheeded. Her maid coming to her room, found her lying upon the ground. Hastily she summoned Diogenes and, together, they laid her upon her couch.

The next morning, Irene was too ill to rise. Several days passed, but her strength returned not.

It was the morning of the twentieth, Diogenes entered her room. Advancing toward his child with cautious tread, he laid his hand upon her forehead and spoke:

"My daughter, you appear somewhat stronger, do you feel better?"

"I feel much stronger, father."

"Can you bear what I have to say?"

"Speak, father."

"My child, the Sultan is expected here to-night."

"To-night!" ejaculated the girl.

"Yes, a courier has arrived in breathless haste, announcing the monarch's approach. The entire castle is in commotion, and innumerable preparations are being made for his reception."

"God help us!" exclaimed Irene.

"Will you not accede to my proposition?"

Irene made no reply.

"Think of your poor brother, your suffering father."

The girl wept in silence.

"Irene have pity on us, I ask you to do nothing wrong. Promise me that you will accede to the Sultan's request, if you find you can do so without sin."

"Father, I cannot promise; give me time."

"Time is short, my dear, the Sultan's wrath is terrible."

"Fear not those that kill the body," answered the girl.

The door was suddenly burst open, a Turk entered, accompanied by a man whose face indicated that he was of Grecian origin, though he was clad in the Turkish costume. The latter spoke in Greek:

"John Diogenes, the hour of your deliverance is at hand; prepare to follow us at midnight, we shall meet you in this room, leave the door open."

"What snares are being laid for us?" cried Diogenes.

"No snares at all. We are friends. Say not a word

of this to a mortal or you shall die. Do you not know Nicolaus Lecapenos ? He will be your deliverer."

"This is more than I can believe." Grasping the man's hand, he cried out: "Friend, friend, is it true ? Will Nicolaus save us ?"

"Hush," said the other, "not so loud. Nicolaus will save you."

"Brave youth! Do you hear, Irene ?"

She spoke not.

"But," asked Diogenes, "what if the Sultan arrives first ?"

"The Sultan is not expected until morning. You have understood us ?"

"Yes, we shall be in readiness."

The men, one of whom was Ali, disguised as a workman, left the room.

The day sped onward in its course, mid hopes and fears. A vessel was beating against the wind in the Ægean Sea. Since early morning it had been obliged to tack, in order to make a little progress, but it was still several miles from the Hellespont. Calm and adverse winds had, thus far, retarded it. Dimitrios paced the deck in the height of nervous agitation. From time to time, he would stop, gaze at the sails, or fix his eyes in the direction of the straits. He was clad in complete armor. At the bow of the vessel two men stood in earnest conversation; they were Selim and Fortuny. The former was still clad as a Turk, but the latter wore a full suit of steel. Some distance from them, two men, steel from head to foot, walked, arm in arm. We recognize Morosini and the fugitive from Constantinople whose narrative had so alarmed Dimitrios and whom Providence had brought on board this vessel in his hope of obtaining a passage to the Islands. He had offered his services to Selim. The crew consisted of six men, besides the captain. Indomitable courage was stamped upon the features of each; they were adventurers from different countries in Europe. The ship on which they sailed was a corsair, but, this time, at least, she was on an honorable expedition.

Hours wore away, but the wind changed not. Darkness was beginning to cover the face of the deep. The impatience of Dimitrios was at its height. They had now reached the mouth of the Hellespont. At the entrance to the straits, a fair breeze sprung up, which swelled the sails and the vessel flew over the waters of the Hellespont.

"Thank God!" gasped Dimitrios.

It was eleven o'clock at night when they arrived at the point indicated by the old woman. The huge towers of the castle arose like grim sentinels in the darkness, rendering the waters still blacker by their shadows.

"There within those walls," said Dimitrios to Morosini, "languishes Irene; I will save her or die!"

The friends grasped each others hands in silence. Two boats were lowered. Into the first stepped Dimitrios, Morosini, Selim, Fortuny, two sailors and the old woman. The other boat followed with the strange Greek, two sailors, and the captain of the vessel. Helena was left on board in charge of the remaining men of the crew. Noiselessly the muffled oars cleaved the waters. In a short time the boats reached the land, where they were made fast. The men sprang ashore and helped the old woman to land.

"Follow me," she whispered to Selim, as she preceded the company.

All walked after her in single file. Suddenly she stopped, and, taking Selim by the arm, she spoke:

"See you those two men? One of them is, no doubt, Nicolaus; be on your guard."

Selim looked, and, half hidden in the bushes, he saw the dark figures of two persons.

"Halt," he spoke, in little more than a whisper, "lie flat on the ground."

All obeyed the injunction. Taking Morosini, Fortuny and the Greek by the arm, he bade them follow him, half creeping over the ground. They moved toward the rear of the men.

"When you are near enough," spoke Selim, "spring upon them."

Cautiously they advanced. Only a couple of yards separated them from their enemies. There was a rustle among the leaves, one of the men turned. In the twinkling of an eye, Morosini sprang upon him, and felled him to the ground. His companion darted off like an arrow, towards the water.

"Speak not a word," said Morosini, "or you are a dead man."

In a moment Nicolaus was bound hand and foot and gagged. Morosini handed him over to a sailor, who took him to the boat, laying him flat on his back in the bottom of the craft. The wretch was unable to stir.

"Now," said the old woman, "take your positions."

The entire company united; all lay down except Selim, who remained standing where Nicolaus Lecapenos had stood, not far from the subterranean passage to the castle.

While the rescuers of Irene remained on guard outside of the castle, within the walls the deepest silence prevailed. Diogenes and his children sat impatiently awaiting the moment that was to free them from the Turks. They could hear the beating of their hearts. Every sound caused by the creaking of a door, the whistling of the wind or the shrieking of a night-owl, caused them to start. The minutes seemed hours. Finally a soft footstep was heard outside the door, and a subdued voice reached their ears:

"Follow us."

Diogenes arose and, taking his children by the hand, followed in the direction whence the voice came.

"Gently!" spoke the unknown, "let not a sound be heard."

Two hands were laid upon Irene's shoulders and an individual pushed her before him, as he said:

"Quietly! tread lightly. Diogenes, lay your hand on my shoulders, and take your son by the hand. Now, forward, as noiselessly as possible."

Together they groped their way through the corridor, then descended cautiously a flight of stairs, which seemed interminable. They had reached the door which communicated with the subterranean passage; it was open. Irene stood near the threshold, when suddenly the light of a torch fell upon them, and a voice cried:

"Hold, robber; to the rescue, men!"

Half a dozen Turks sprang forward. The man who held Irene released his hold, and started through the subterranean passage. He had escaped.

"Treason!" cried Ali.

"Treason, workman, what treason? Where do you come from at this hour of the night?" asked one of the Turks.

"I heard the sound of voices and footsteps in this direction. Thinking that the Sultan had arrived, curiosity directed me hither. Who would have thought that such things were happening? Where is the traitor?"

"He has escaped," cried a Turk.

Diogenes and his small family were conducted back to their apartments and locked together in a room.

The hour of midnight was approaching; with the greatest anxiety did the party outside of the castle keep their eyes riveted on the spot where they knew the entrance to the subterranean passage lay. At any moment Irene and her would-be-deliverer might come forth. Not an instant did Dimitrios avert his gaze from the spot. The minutes dragged slowly along, his heart thumped within his bosom as though it would force itself out of his breast. Still all was silent, as silent as the tomb. The breeze had died away and not a leaf stirred upon the trees.

"Hist!" whispered Fortuny, "do you hear?"

"There they come!" exclaimed the old woman in a low tone.

"Attention!" spoke Selim.

Suddenly a man sprang as it were out of the ground. In an instant, Morosini was at his side, holding him in an iron grasp. The stranger spoke a few unintelligible words in Turkish. Morosini replied in Greek:

"Move not, if you value your life."

"I am a Greek," replied the stranger in the same language.

"Where do you come from?" asked Morosini.

"From the castle—let me go, they are pursuing me."

Morosini dragged him away from the spot towards his companions.

"What have you done?" he asked, "why are you flying?"

"I was attempting to rescue a Greek maiden from the Turks, but the wretches discovered the plot as we were about to put it into a successful execution."

"Is the maiden still in the castle?"

"Yes, in the power of those brutes, and the Sultan is expected before morning."

"Is there a garrison in the castle?"

"No, it is guarded only by ten men."

"Do you hear, comrades?"

"We hear," sounded the reply.

"What shall we do, brethren?"

Dimitrios had drawn his sword. Raising it above his head, he cried out:

"Forward, brothers, **forward!** Follow me; liberty for Irene, or—death!"

"Be calm, Dimitrios," remonstrated Selim, "let reflection precede action. Men, I advise that we storm the castle. It is true; they are ten, and we are only eight, but we are better equipped."

Turning to the old woman, he said:

"Return to the boat and await us."

"I will await you here," she replied.

To the fugitive from the castle Selim spoke:

"You shall serve us as a guide; but, beware man! if you betray us, you die."

"Betray you? I am too glad to render assistance."

"Get the torches in readiness," cried Selim, "and advance."

Steadily they marched forward. Reaching the entrance to the passage, Morosini took the guide by the arm. The captain of the ship lit a torch, which cast an unearthly glare over the men, and revealed a long, dark passage that lay before them.

"Advance!" cried Selim.

Dimitrios, sword in hand, took the lead. The end of the passage was reached, they ascended a flight of stairs, at the head of which stood a door. It was locked.

"The door is locked!" exclaimed the guide.

"Force it open!" cried Dimitrios.

"To work men, with a will!" shouted Selim.

The two sailors and the ship's captain came forward with huge axes. It was clear that the door opened from the interior.

"Strike away!" cried Dimitrios, impatiently.

The axes swung in the brawny hands of the stalwart tars, they fell against the massive oaken door, which groaned under the shock.

"Courage, men!" exclaimed the captain, "it is yielding."

The blows fell thick and fast.

"It is yielding!" repeated a sailor.

"Bravo!" exclaimed another, as a panel gave way and fell with a loud report that re-echoed through the long dismal corridor, in which even the low voices of the speakers assumed enormous volume. Still the blows fell, another panel was yielding. A confused sound of voices met them from the inside.

"Forward with your torch!" commanded Selim.

As the torch-bearer advanced, a bright light was thrown into the interior, which revealed a Turk rushing down the stairs.

"Forward. my men!" yelled Dimitrios, as he forced his way through the broken door, followed by the others.

No sooner had the Turk beheld the armed men before him, than he halted, as if thunderstruck.

"Come on, son of Belial," Dimitrios fairly screamed.

The Turk turned on his heels and ran up the stairway, shouting at the top of his voice. Dimitrios was after him, taking two steps at a time, and crying:

"Follow, brothers, follow. Here Byzantium, down with the infidels, down with Mahomet!"

"Hold, Dimitrios! do not separate from the rest," Selim's voice sounded.

"Lead the way," cried Morosini to the guide.

"This way, countrymen, this way, up the stairs."

Up the stairs they rushed. Dimitrios had outrun them in his eagerness. They heard the clash of arms.

"Forward!" cried Selim.

As they reached the head of the stairs, they saw Dimitrios, surrounded by several Mussulmans. With his shield he parried the blows of their scimitars, while he wielded his broadsword with deadly effect. One man lay already writhing upon the ground. As the Turks beheld the reinforcement arrive above the head of the stairs, they retreated toward the door where Diogenes and his family were locked, while the Greeks pressed hard upon them. With their backs to the door, the Turks fought furiously.

"Surrender your prisoners," cried in the Turkish tongue Selim, who stood in the background without taking part in the fray.

"Never!" replied the chieftain of the Turks.

"Then die, wretch," cried Dimitrios, as he cast himself upon the Mahometan, who, by a skillful movement, evaded the sword of his antagonist, which stuck into the wood of the door. The Turk raised his scimitar above the head of Dimitrios, who dexterously received the blow upon his shield, and, at the same time, disengaging his sword from the wood, thrust it through the body of the unfortunate chieftain, who fell without a groan. The Turks, seeing this, rushed simultaneously upon Dimitrios. His comrades closed in around him. Swords clashed with swords, the blows of the Turks fell almost harmless upon the armored bodies of the Greeks, but one of the sailors lay wounded upon the ground. The other one, a young Genoese, fought like a lion. Seeing a Turk making a movement as if to sever the head of Morosini, he rushed upon him, caught his arm, and plunged a dagger into his breast.

"Bravo, Cristoforo!" cried the captain.

A Turk rushed wildly upon Fortuny. The latter, parrying the blow of his scimitar, caught him around the waist and flung him to the ceiling, whence he fell with a heavy thud to the ground.

"Surrender!" again cried Selim.

The Turks, seeing that resistance was useless, as only four of their number were left to fight against six, most of whom were armored, threw down their swords and cried for quarter. They were immediately surrounded by the Greeks, who demanded the keys of the apartment. They hung upon the girdle of the dead chieftain. The swords of the Turks were now collected together by young Cristoforo, so that they might be rendered harmless.

"Who will open the door?" asked Dimitrios, adding:

"I would rather not go in too suddenly, lest the shock might prove injurious to Irene."

Morosini took the key, unlocked the door, and pushed it open. Irene knelt upon the ground, trembling with fear, while her eyes were raised to Heaven. Her father stood erect, gazing at the entrance, while Basil clung to him, as though fearful of being dragged away by force.

"Rejoice, Diogenes," said Morosini, "thy deliverance has been effected, thou art free, follow us without delay."

"Who art thou?" inquired the prisoner.

"It matters not, thou wilt soon know; I am a Christian and a friend, lose no time."

Taking Irene and Basil by the hand, Diogenes walked out of the room in which they had been locked. The Turks lay bound upon the ground, while their dead comrades were scattered around them.

"They are harmless now," said the captain of the ship, giving one of them a kick.

Placing the rescued captives in the middle, and raising their wounded comrade, the victors descended the stairs, walked through the subterranean passage, and passed out into the open air. The old woman, who had been anxiously awaiting them, ran towards them, exclaiming:

"Thank God, they have been successful!"

"Lose no time," cried Selim, "to the boats!"

On reaching the landing, they placed Diogenes and his children, with two sailors, in charge of Morosini, while the others sprang into the boat in which lay Nicolaus. The return to the vessel was made in perfect silence; no one spoke a word and no sound broke the stillness of the night, save the dipping of the oars into the water. The hull of the ship lay motionless upon the placid waters, no breath stirred the lifeless atmosphere.

They had reached the deck; Selim approached the group, consisting of the family of Diogenes and Morosini.

"Let us thank God, gentle lady," he said, "for your deliverance out of the hands of the infidel."

Irene fell upon her knees and, for a few moments, remained in silent prayer; then she arose, cast herself upon her father's breast, giving vent to tears and sobs, indicative of her emotion.

"You need rest," spoke Selim, "will you allow us to conduct you to the cabin?"

Meanwhile, the captain's voice was heard giving orders to the crew; oars were put out, as the sails were useless in the calm, and the ship headed for the Ægean Sea.

"Where is Nicolaus Lecapenos?" asked Diogenes, "may we not express our thanks to him?"

"Nicolaus," replied Selim, "is a prisoner on this vessel; he deserves no thanks."

"Nicolaus a prisoner! deserves no thanks! What mystery is this? Is not Nicolaus our deliverer?"

"You are mistaken, noble sir, you owe not your deliverance to Nicolaus, but to another, with whom you are acquainted, a heroic son of Byzantium!"

"To whom?" exclaimed Irene, "tell us his name, that we may cast ourselves at his feet."

"You know him, lady, you esteem him highly."

"I know him? I esteem him? Keep me not in suspense, I pray."

"Lady, sudden joy may prove as injurious as sudden grief."

"But suspense is worse than death."

"Your deliverer is dear to you, suspect you not who he is?"

"Where is our deliverer?" cried the maiden, "let us see him."

"Suspect you not who he is?"

"I dare not give expression to my thoughts; there is one, who, I know, would risk his life for me."

"And that one is—?"

"Alas! I dare not hope it is he, the disappointment would be my death."

"Perhaps you are not mistaken. Know you the family of Phocas?"

"Am I right? Oh, tell me, is it Dimitrios?"

"You have said it, lady, Dimitrios Phocas is your deliverer."

"Oh, where is he?" cried the girl, "where is Dimittrios, why does he not come forward?"

The figure of a man advanced in the darkness.

"Hold, Irene!" cried her father, "I suspect there has been treachery. Why is Nicolaus a prisoner?"

"There has been treachery," replied Selim, "black, infernal treachery, but not on the part of Dimitrios. You will soon know all, and then you will make amends for your credulity."

Irene, paying no attention to what was said, again cried out:

"Oh, bring Dimitrios to me!"

"There is Dimitrios," said Selim, as the youth advanced.

Irene flew to him; Dimitrios knelt before her, and taking one of her hands, kissed it, saying:

"God be praised, my lady Eiréné, thou art restored to me. Dost thou still believe me guilty?"

"Believe thee guilty, Dimitrios? When did I believe thee guilty? The rocks might split asunder, the sun lose its light and the stars their splendor, but Eiréné's heart would never believe in thy guilt."

"Oh, thanks, a thousand thanks! I knew it was a calumny cast upon thy love."

"Arise, Dimitrios, kneel not to me, rather should I cast myself upon my knees before thee. But, tell me, who did thus calumniate me?"

"Who? One who is now a prisoner on this vessel."

"Nicolaus? The wretch!"

"Yes, Irene, it was Nicolaus, the holy pilgrim."

"Great God!" exclaimed Diogenes, "a light arises before me; what mystery of iniquity is here? Dimitrios, I have wronged thee, explain and ease my heart."

"Not to-night, father," answered the youth, "take first your rest, to-morrow you shall know all."

Irene was now conducted to the after part of the ship, covered by a roof, which served as a cabin. As her eyes fell upon Helena, she rushed to the girl's arms, exclaiming:

"Oh, my sister, my long lost sister, this joy is too great for earth!"

The two girls fell into each other's arms and wept in silence.

When the first rays of dawn illumined the horizon, they found the vessel sailing before the wind on the blue waters of the Ægean Sea. Diogenes was up before the sun. Immediately he sought Selim, whom he found with Morosini. From the lips of the latter, he heard, with sorrow in his soul, the story of the treachery of Nicolaus, the murder of Leila, the escape of Lecapenos, and the incidents of the rescue.

"I will to him at once," said Diogenes, "I will kneel at his feet, I will implore his pardon."

As he spoke, a young woman approached the group from a remote corner of the vessel. It was her first appearance on board; all eyes were turned upon her. A shriek was heard, proceeding from the bow of the vessel:

"Save me, save me! It is her ghost!"

As Diogenes turned, he beheld Nicolaus, bound hand and foot, lying on the deck, with his head raised, and his eyes, starting from their sockets, intently fixed upon the approaching figure of the woman.

Morosini had not removed his gaze from her:

"It is she," he spoke, "it is her spirit, the spirit of Angela."

"No, not a spirit," replied the woman, "it is Angela herself, Angela Ladrazzoni, the unfortunate Leila, now a repentant Magdalene."

Morosini could not believe his eyes.

"Be not astonished," she continued, "it is I. My life has been spared for a wise purpose. You thought me dead; I live. My wound, though dangerous, was not mortal; the ministrations of a Good Samaritan brought me back from the border of the tomb. I was the old woman whom Providence sent as an instrument for the deliverance of Irene."

"Wretch," cried Selim, as he turned toward Nicolaus, "did I not tell thee that thy tool might some day cut thee?"

"There," exclaimed Angela, as she pointed toward the unfortunate man, "there is the guilty one, whose calumny brought untold sorrow upon a happy family, the monster who ruined my life, then steeped his hands in my blood. There is the guilty one, Dimitrios is innocent."

"Father in Heaven," exclaimed Diogenes, "why did'ts Thou permit it!"

Within a few moments the contrite man had cast himself before Dimitrios, imploring his forgiveness. The latter raised him up and embraced him, as he spoke:

"My father, let all be buried in the grave of the past."

Diogenes summoned his daughter, and placing her hand in that of her betrothed, spoke:

"My children, God has united you, you belong to each other."

Irene's eyes fell, as she slowly pronounced the words:
"In eternity."

CHAPTER XXV.

Joy reigned on board the ship. Days of darkness and terror were at an end. Although it was with feelings of horror, that those who had witnessed the fall of Constantinople, looked back upon the bloody scenes that had there been enacted, the present contained so much of joy that it forced the sorrowful to the background, for in present happiness man is prone to forget that which was bitter in the past. However, this picture had also its shade. Sullen and gloomy, Nicolaus gazed upon the joy of those whom he considered his enemies. The old hatred against Dimitrios had returned to his heart with renewed force, and, concentrated within himself, he seemed to be brooding over new plans of revenge. Dimitrios, prompted by the generous impulses of his heart, had endeavored to enter into conversation with the unfortunate man, but he was every time repulsed by the wretch who turned away his face from him.

Nothing at first occurred to disturb the pleasure of the voyage; the sea was calm, and a light breeze impelled the vessel, which, with her white sails filled by the wind, seemed an immense swan floating over the peaceful waters. She passed the Turkish galleys in safety, protected by the standard of the Moorish kingdom of Grenada, which floated from her mast-head. Off the coast of Troas, Dimitrios pointed out to Irene and Helena, the direction, where, some miles from the sea, lay the ancient city of Troy, celebrated in Homeric legends, and, as he recalled its fate, he could not help paying the tribute of a tear to his own loved city of Byzantium. Leaving the western coast of Asia Minor, they sailed partly around the Island of Mitylene, and headed directly for the channel between Scio and the coast of Ionia; thence passing to the west of Samos, they reached Patmos, renowned as the spot where St. John the Evangelist was privileged to behold the wonderful visions of the Apocalypse.

It was a bright afternoon. The sky was nearly cloudless, the sea barely ruffled by the breeze, and all nature seemed to breathe peace and tranquility, so different from the fierce passions that were animating the human breast in various countries of the known globe. A flock of land birds soared high in the heavens, while an occasional sea-gull hovered around the ship, forming semicircles in the air, and, again dipping into the water. The happy group sat upon the deck in admiration of the scene.

"How lovely," spoke Selim, "must not the sojourn of St. John have been upon yonder island! Far from the bustle and turmoil of the world, he might give himself over to the delights of contemplation. With what longing I look forward to my monastic home! Divine Providence has afforded me this opportunity of escape, I will not reject it, for I consider that my mission among the Turks is at an end. Henceforth I am Selim no longer, I am Father Gregorio again, and, as soon as possible, I will once more clothe myself in my monastic habit."

"Why not immediately, Father Gregorio?" asked Helena, "Irene and myself will make you a habit. Show us how it is made."

The religious, pleased with this offer, sketched for the

girls the habit of the Order of Mercy, and the two ladies, full of enthusiasm, immediately set to work. The ship was ransacked in all directions for the required material. The captain, though a Mohamedan, lent them aid, and a few yards of white flannel were discovered. Work was immediately begun, continued and even protracted far into the night. Finally the task was accomplished, and, the next morning, Father Gregorio appeared on deck in the white robes of his Order, with the arms of Arragon on his breast, to the great surprise of the crew, and the delight of his friends. Nicolaus gazed at him with mingled wonder and rage. Irene had learned of the conversion of Dimitrios and Helena, and she, too, had placed herself under the instructions of Father Gregorio, determined to embrace the faith of the Latins, if she could be persuaded. Her father, however, held aloof. Time passed pleasantly away. Dimitrios, touched with compassion at the miserable condition of Nicolaus, had persuaded his companions to loosen his fetters, although he was rendered harmless by the constant vigilance of two sailors whom the captain had placed over him as a guard. The ship was now off the most south-western point of Asia Minor, at only a few miles distance from the land, and running before the wind. It was a clear and starlit night. The passengers were on the deck in various groups, Dimitrios and Morosini in earnest conversation, while Father Gregorio entertained Irene and Helena on the primacy of the Roman Pontiff. Suddenly a man rushed toward the stern of the vessel; in an instant two sailors were in hot pursuit, but they were too late. With the velocity of a deer, chased by the hounds, the fugitive bounded up the ladder to the after deck. Without arresting his progress, he cried in a loud voice:

"Farewell, Irene, farewell forever; Nicolaus seeks rest beneath the waves!"

As the last word was uttered, he stood at the stern of the ship—Dimitrios rushed forward, Nicolaus threw up his hands, his body leaned forward, he had disappeared. As he vanished over the side he was heard to exclaim again:

"Farewell, Irene, farewell forever!"

The ship lay to, a boat was lowered, but all search proved in vain. The darkness of night covered the waves. An hour was spent without result, and finally the search was abandoned. Such was the fate of the unhappy being who had wrecked his life, for the gratification of his passions. Dimitrios mourned sincerely the loss of the unfortunate man, and Angela shed a tear for him who had been her greatest enemy, while she prayed God to have mercy on his soul.

Finding that the search had been useless, the captain ordered the ship to hold to her course, and she headed directly for the Island of Rhodes. During the night the wind changed, and it became necessary to tack in order to reach the port. When day dawned, the vessel lay in full view of the famous island, then in possession of the Knights Hospitallers of St. John of Jerusalem. Thinking it might be dangerous to enter this Christian port with the flag of the Moors, the captain hailed a passing vessel and sent word to the authorities on shore that he carried Christian refugees from Constantinople. Meanwhile he lay to, awaiting an answer.

Dimitrios and Morosini leaned against the bulwarks, looking toward the island; on the after deck sat Helena and Irene. The latter appeared pale and languid. Father Gregorio was reciting his office, while Fortuny entertained the Greek from Constantinople with narratives of his travels and adventures. Angela was engaged in preparing refreshments for Irene, to whom she was most assiduous in her attentions.

"What an extraordinary island!" exclaimed Dimitrios, as he fixed his eyes upon the land.

"Yes," replied Morosini, "it has had a wonderful history. It was once the most renowned state in Greece, and, after the death of Alexander the Great, its magnificence was unsurpassed and it took its place among the most warlike nations of the world. It formed a part of the Roman Empire until the reign of Andronicus II, at the end of the thirteenth and the beginning of the last century. The nobles having revolted, invoked the Saracens, who occupied the island until 1309. Foulques de Villaret was then Grand-Master of the Order of St. John, which had its headquarters in Cyprus; he called upon the Emperor Andronicus at Constantinople, and the latter gave him the investiture of the island for himself and his order, on condition that he should wrest it from the infidels. Pope Clement V. confirmed this donation and aided the Knights in the conquest of the island. On August 15, 1309, the island fell into the hands of the Knights, who have held it ever since. It was several times besieged by the Mahometans, namely, in 1310, in 1321, and in 1444, but always unsuccessfully. The capital, also called Rhodes, is strongly fortified and well-nigh impregnable."

In the midst of these conversations, the day passed away, until about two o'clock in the afternoon, when signals were perceived, made by a vessel that lay between them and the land.

"We may enter the harbor," cried the captain.

The ship which had been sailing to and fro before the island, now swung around and headed directly for the harbor. In a short while the immense walls of the city stood before them, and objects on shore became distinctly visible. The vessel cast anchor, boats were lowered, and the Christian travelers, having bade farewell to the captain, whom Selim amply rewarded, stepped into them. As they approached near to the shore, Dimitrios, pointing with his finger, asked of Morosini:

"Who is that man in the black robe, with an eight-pointed white cross on the left side?"

"He is one of the Knights," answered Morosini, "the eight-pointed cross is the distinctive mark of the order."

"Can you tell me who is at present the Grand-Master?"

"His name is John de Lassie. He is a native of Auvergne, in France, and he has been Grand-Master for twenty-two years, which dignity was conferred upon him after the death of his predecessor, Antonio Flurian, that occurred in 1431."

They had now reached the shore, where several Knights were drawn up in line to welcome the fugitives and hear of the fall of Constantinople. The newcomers were pressed by questions on all sides, to which they gladly responded. One of the most distinguished of the Knights, a Grand Cross of the Order, offered to procure a house for the entire party, which offer was most thankfully accepted, and, in a short time, all found themselves comfortably lodged in a spacious dwelling.

Towards evening, Father Gregorio, Morosini and Dimitrios paid their respects to the Grand-Master and to the Archbishop. Both these dignitaries listened with the greatest interest to their recital of the exciting and terrible events of the last few months.

The next morning the company were astir at an early hour, but one of the number was missing. When Dimitrios entered the room where they were gathered, after the first salutation his eyes wandered around, but they rested not on an object they sought.

"She is not here yet," said Helena, laughing.

Dimitrios endeavored to conceal his disappointment and seated himself, joining in the conversation. Time passed, but Irene appeared not.

"Where can Irene be?" finally exclaimed her father.

"No doubt she is tired from journeying and in need of rest," replied Helena, "I will go to her room."

As she ran out of the apartment, she met at the door Angela, who exclaimed:

"Come quickly, quickly, the lady Irene is ill."

Without a word, Helena rushed to the girl's room. As she entered, she drew back astonished. Irene's face wore a crimson hue, her eyes were glassy, and they had a peculiar stare in them.

"Irene, my dear, what ails thee?" asked the sister of Dimitrios, in a sympathetic tone.

Putting her hand to her forehead, she replied:

"My head, oh, my head!"

"I will send for your father."

"Yes," whispered the sick girl.

Angela ran to the room where the company was gathered, and whispered something to Diogenes, who, at once, arose and left the apartment, while Dimitrios followed him uneasily with his eyes.

A physician was at once sent for. On his arrival, he declared that, in consequence of the terrible mental strain she had gone through, the poor girl was prostrated. At the present moment she was in a burning fever. It is impossible to imagine the alarm that seized Dimitrios, when this announcement was made to him; but the declaration of the physician that the indisposition would, probably, pass away in a few days, was a star of hope. Days went, but Irene was no better— Dimitrios implored God to restore his betrothed to health, but his prayer remained unanswered. On the fifth morning after their arrival at Rhodes, gloom seemed to have settled over the household, and the face of each one was overcast by a cloud. Dimitrios had just returned from a church dedicated to the Mother of God, where he had received the Holy Communion. As he entered the house, he was met by Angela, who thus addressed him:

"The lady Irene desires to speak to you."

In an instant he was at her door. Being admitted into the room, he found her father seated beside her. Except the light of a feeble lamp, which cast a dim reflection over the countenance of Irene Diogenes, the room was in darkness. It seemed to Dimitrios as though the shadows of death had, already, been cast over the apartment. In silence he knelt beside the patient, she fixed her eyes upon him and smiled, then, in a feeble voice, spoke :

"Dimitrios, be not sad; remember, we are Christians."

"Oh, Irene! what wilt thou say to me?"

"Be seated, Dimitrios, and listen."

The youth did as she bade him, while tears moistened his eyelids; Diogenes held his eyes fixed upon his daughter. The girl continued:

"Dimitrios, hast thou heard the verdict of the physician?"

He answered not, but, burying his face in his hands, wept like a child.

"Weep not, Dimitrios, is not life a sad dream?"

The youth cast himself upon his knees, exclaiming:

"O God, my God! this is too hard to bear, to suffer shipwreck in the very harbor!"

"Speak not thus, Dimitrios, arise from thy knees and calm thy agitation."

Young Phocas again seated himself, while Irene continued:

"My dearest brother, thus will I call thee forever, our parting will be only for a short time. I go hence to a land where peace perpetual reigns, but thou wilt follow me. I know that human skill has exhausted its efforts. I feel that life is ebbing, but before I go, I will take a step which will compensate thee for my loss. God's light shines before my eyes, I will return to the faith my fathers abandoned—my doubts have vanished, and it seems as though the brightness of the Eternal Vision already casts its reflection over my soul. We have informed the Archbishop of my resolution. He knows our history and he will come himself to receive me into the bosom of the Church. Oh, the joy of that blessed moment!"

The inspiration of the dying girl was such that her supernatural happiness communicated itself to the heart of Dimitrios, and helped to dispel the darkness of his sorrowing soul, which was being purified in the crucible of the most dire affliction. The Archbishop was expected to arrive within an hour. The room of Irene had been adorned for the occasion. Dimitrios noticed now for the first time, so absorbed had his attention been, that a table with a crucifix and candles had been prepared for the reception of the Holy Eucharist. Bouquets of the choicest flowers were tastefully arranged around the apartment, while a most delicate perfume spread itself over the air.

At the appointed time, the tinkling of a bell announced the approach of the Blessed Sacrament, borne by the Archbishop under a canopy of white silk, held by four clerics, while others preceded him with lighted tapers in their hands. At the sound of the bell, Dimitrios and Diogenes fell upon their knees. As the ecclesiastics accompanying the Blessed Sacrament entered the room, they were followed by Father Gregorio, Morosini, Fortuny and Angela. All knelt down, nor was there a dry eye in the apartment. The piety of Dimitrios showed itself in his whole demeanor, but the grief stamped upon his features was pitiful in the extreme.

The Archbishop, having placed the sacred Pyxis upon the corporal, turned toward Irene, and, in a fatherly voice, asked her in Latin, with which the sick girl was familiar:

"My daughter, dost thou believe in God, the Father Almighty, the Creator of Heaven and earth?"

The reply sounded in a low but firm tone:

"*Credo*, I believe."

"Dost thou believe in Jesus Christ, His only Son our Lord, who suffered and who was crucified?"

"*Credo*."

"Dost thou believe in the Holy Ghost, the Holy Catholic Church, the communion of saints, the forgiveness of sins, the resurrection of the body and the life everlasting?"

Irene's face brightened, her eyes sparkled, a halo seemed to surround her as she answered:

"*Credo.*"

"Dost thou believe that the Holy Ghost proceedeth from the Father and the Son?"

"*Credo.*"

"Believest thou in the supremacy of jurisdiction of the Bishop of Rome, the successor of St. Peter, the Vicar of Christ?"

"*Credo, credo, firmissime credo*—I believe, I believe, I believe most firmly," cried the girl, with energy.

The Prelate knowing that, although the physician had declared the girl could not recover, still death was not imminent, had asked for the edification of those present, these questions which, otherwise, might have been reduced to very few words.

One of the assistants now recited the confession or *confiteor*, and the Bishop, turning to the girl, absolved her from all censure, in virtue of the authority delegated to him by the Sovereign Pontiff. The prelate, in company of all present, now withdrew, leaving alone with Irene a venerable friar of the order of St. Francis, a man well versed in the Greek tongue. They waited outside until her confession was finished. It lasted a short time, for, no doubt, grievous sin had never blighted the virginal flower that seemed about to be transplanted from earth to Paradise, and Irene, who was well instructed, could, with the aid of her confessor, sum up her transgressions in a few words. When the friar came forth, the Archbishop and the other persons re-entered the room. The solemn moment had now arrived, the priestly hand held the Sacred Host, upon which the eyes of Irene were riveted. As though moved by an inspiration, the Archbishop spoke:

"Child of God, thou beholdest Him now in a cloud and in obscurity, thou soon shalt see Him as He is."

"*Facie ad faciem*, from face to face," added Irene.

"*Ecce Agnus Dei !* Behold the Lamb of God, that taketh away the sins of the world," spoke the Bishop; then, approaching the girl and making the sign of the Cross with the Sacred Host, he pronounced the words:

"Receive, sister, the Viaticum of the Body of our Lord Jesus Christ, and may it preserve thee from the wicked enemy and lead thee to eternal life. Amen."

The head of Dimitrios was deeply bowed, tears coursed down his cheeks. How awful was that moment! Perfect resignation filled his heart, but it was the resignation of Gethsemane. In the depths of his soul he prayed:

"Father, if it be possible, let the chalice pass," but, he added, too: "not my will, but thine be done."

Irene had now received her first Holy Communion after her union with the great body of the faithful, and happiness beamed from every feature of her countenance. The Sacrament of Extreme Unction was now administered to her, while the assistants recited the Penitential Psalms. The ceremony was over, all left the room, save Diogenes, who still knelt beside his daughter. For a long time Irene prayed in silence. Finally, laying her hand upon her father's head, she spoke:

"Father, promise me one thing, and I will die happy."

"I promise all, my child," he replied, in tears.

"Promise that you will endeavor to follow my example, or, at least, that you will try to find the truth, and, having found it, that you will have the courage to embrace it."

"You have my word, Irene, and you know how faithful that word is."

"Oh, thanks, thanks, dear father! now may I depart hence in peace."

The day passed away, but there was no change in the patient's condition. Dimitrios visited her as often as possible, while Helena never left her bedside.

The next morning there was a marked improvement. The girl's voice was stronger, her pains had decreased and she rested more quietly. A ray of light streamed into the household; for the first time in several days a smile passed over those who moved noiselessly about. Reader, did you ever notice the flame of a candle that is nearing its end? Gradually it grows fainter, then, suddenly, it brightens up as if to bid farewell; for a moment it shines with unwonted brilliancy, then the brightness wanes, until it goes over into darkness. Was it thus with Irene?

Certainly there had been an improvement. But, alas! how vain are human hopes! The afternoon came, and, with it a change for the worst. Diogenes sat beside his daughter.

"Father," she spoke, "send for Dimitrios."

Within a few moments the heart-broken young man knelt beside the bed of her to whom his heart clung, but whom death was fast separating from him. If ever you visit Westminster Abbey, reader, fail not to see the chapel of St. John the Evangelist. There you will find a monument to Joseph Gascoigne Nightingale and his

Lady. As I write of the sorrows of Dimitrios, that monument comes back vividly to my mind. The lady is represented expiring in the arms of her husband; grim Death, creeping from a tomb, points his dart at her, while the husband, struck with despair, endeavors to shield her against the attack of the foe. Dimitrios had lost all hope, and yet, oh, how ardently he would have snatched Irene from the enemy! but, who can resist death? The brave young soldier had stood in the front ranks of the defenders of a large city, and now he is powerless to defend her whom he loves best.

Turning her dying eyes upon him, Irene spoke:

"Dimitrios, are you resigned?"

He raised his eyes to Heaven, and with clasped hands, pronounced the words:

"Father, Thy will be done!"

"There," said Irene, as she pointed her finger upward, "there we shall meet, to part no more. There shall be no sorrow, nor sickness, nor pain, nor death. I have lived as the roses live, the brief space of a morning, for what else has been my life? Yet, I die happy, for I am going to our true country, I am going to await you in the bosom of an endless rest."

Dimitrios could not utter a word, his emotion choked him. His sister knelt beside him, bathed in tears. Casting her eyes upon her, Irene spoke:

"Helena, summon the others."

Basil was already in the room, kneeling beside the bed with his head leaning upon his sister's hand, speechless with grief. The other inmates of the house were in the vicinity. At the first summons, they entered the chamber of death and knelt around the couch. Irene's dying voice sounded:

"My friends, I am going home, not to Byzantium that I shall never see again on earth, but to Jerusalem, the city of eternal peace. I am going, but you will all soon follow me; envy me not my happiness—soon I shall see God. Is not this promised to the pure in heart? See God! Oh, the ineffable delight! As a mariner towards the end of his journey catches sight of the land, before he enters the harbor, thus do I catch a glimpse of the promised land. You are still too far away to see the things I see, and hear the things I hear. To see God, and contemplate the Infinite, the always new and always old, the first cause and last end of all things, the source of all that is and all that moves, the Prototype of this vast and glorious universe, to be plunged in a shoreless ocean of ineffable delight without fear of losing it, to find new joys in every moment of an endless duration; such is the bliss in store for me. Farewell earth, thy joys sink into insignifigance. As the stars vanish before the brightness of the rising sun, thus vanish earthly joys of time before thy radiant light, eternity. Farewell, friends, once more, it is only for a brief period. Farewell, sweet Basil, my brother, be faithful to your God; farewell father, I will remember you before the Throne; and thou, Helena, my sister, death shall not part us. Farewell, Dimitrios, we believe in the communion of saints, we have loved each other here, the tomb is only a bridge, my spirit shall hover over you. I come, my God, I come. Let thy servant depart in peace,"

The voice of Irene was silent, her eyelids drooped, her breathing became heavier. Father Gregorio began the prayers for the agonizing, which were joined in by all present, mid tears and sobs. In voices broken by grief, the response was repeated at the litany.

"Pray for her," resounded mid the shadows of the tomb.

"Go forth, O, Christian soul!" said the priest, "in the name of God, the Father Almighty, who created thee; in the name of Jesus Christ the Son of the Living God, who suffered for thee; in the name of the Holy Ghost, who has been poured upon thee."

He stopped, cast his eyes upon her, and listened attentively. Her breathing had ceased. He arose, approached the bed, and raised her hand; it fell back lifeless. The girl had fallen asleep—asleep into that slumber whence there is no awakening until the day when the grave shall surrender its dead. Her soul had winged its flight to God. The priest fell upon his knees as he repeated the words:

"Eternal rest, give unto her, O, Lord! and let perpetual light shine upon her."

"Oh, my child, my darling child!" cried Diogenes, as he threw himself upon the face of the corpse, "my child, hast thou left thy father?"

Basil broke out in loud sobs, Helena buried her face in her hands and wept in silence; even Fortuny shed tears. Dimitrios arose; he was an altered man. Firmness was depicted upon every feature of his countenance.

"Desist, my friends," he cried, "the girl is not dead, but sleepeth. Even at this moment, Irene is looking down upon us from the bosom of a blessed eternity. We believe in the communion of saints. She told us we soon should follow. A short time, and we will be with Irene. Till then Dimitrios will patiently wait—he will never wed, for he can never love as he loved Irene."

The frame of the young man drew itself up to its full height, he looked like an inspired prophet in the dim glare of the light that illumined the abode of death. With a clear and sonorous voice, he exclaimed:

"By the bier of her I loved, there is no room for revenge; but," drawing his sword and holding it above his head, he added: "henceforth my life is consecrated to the service of the Church and of society. The Byzantine Empire has fallen, but the great Christian Empire lasts; to it this sword belongs—I join the military order of St. John of Jerusalem. Irene, thy voice is silent, but I shall hear it still. I shall hear it mid the silence of the night; I shall hear it mid the din of battle. It will lead me on to deeds of virtue, to deeds of heroism, and, when death's shadows gather round me, thy voice, Irene, will bid me welcome to a better fatherland, thy voice shall call me home."

EPILOGUE.

Twenty-seven years have passed since the virginal body of Irene Diogenes, clad in white robes, emblematic of her innocence, was laid in its coffin. It reposes beneath a simple marble slab, on which the traveler may read the inscription, in Greek letters:

Eiréné.

Not a day has gone by, but it has been visited by Dimitrios, who is now a professed Knight of Rhodes, faithful to the vow he took beside the corpse of Irene. He has distinguished himself among his brethren, being now a member of the Council of the Grand Master, and, consequently, a Grand Cross of the Order. He has attached himself to the language or province of Venice, as he feels, since the fall of Constantinople, that the country of Morosini is nearer to him than any other.

Great changes have taken place since the mournful day when the different characters of our story were gathered together in the death-chamber, where lay the body of Irene. John Diogenes, faithful to his word, renounced the Greek schism, and returned to the bosom of the universal Church. He survived his daughter a very few years, and died at Rhodes, in the arms of Dimitrios, and he has gone to rejoin Irene in the bosom of God. His son, Basil, who had learned the inconstancy of human things at an early period of life, has abandoned the world, and he is now a Friar of the Order of Our Lady of Mount Carmel at Mantua. Angela Ladrazzoni, touched with compunction at the frailties of her early life, and disgusted with the world, now serves God in a monastery of nuns of the Order of Citeaux, in the diocese of Limoges in France, where she weeps in the silence of the cloister over the sorrows she caused Dimitrios, and awaits patiently the day that will deliver her soul from its captivity. Father Gregorio, now a venerable man, bent under the weight of years, still lives in the retirement of his monastic home in Spain, and often does his memory wander to scenes of long ago, and do familiar faces arise before him. He keeps up a loving correspondence with his old friend Dimitrios. Fortuny, after a life of countless vicissitudes, abandoned his wanderings and returned to his home, where he died as a true Christian, in sentiments of great piety. Morosini and Helena are still among the living, united by the sacred ties of matrimony. Their happy home is in the Palazzo Morosini, on the Grand Canal at Venice, near the old wooden bridge, where, in the future, the fine Rialto will span the canal. As by moonlight, they float in their gondola, while the soft notes of the mandolin are wafted over the waters, they love to relate to their little ones the tales of days long past, and speak of their Uncle Dimitrios on the far-off Island of Rhodes.

All attempts at union with the Latin Church have ceased at Constantinople, and the wish of old Notaras has been verified: the turban of the Turk is there and not the Pope's tiara. Mahomet II. still reigns; he is determined to subject Rhodes, and he has sworn that he will cut off the head of the Grand-Master with his own hand. He will fail.

*   *   *   *   *   *   *

A beautiful day in the early part of the year 1482, is drawing to a close. It is nearly thirty years since first we met, reader, in the shadow of St. Sophia's Dome at Constantinople; another Byzantine dome reflects the sun's light upon us this evening, that of St. Mark's at Venice. Numberless pedestrians stroll about the Piazza di San Marco before the sacred edifice, children amuse themselves feeding the flocks of tame pigeons that have taken possession of the great square, while merchants exhibit their heterogenous wares in the various booths under the arcades. All seems animated with a common feeling of restful joy at the end of the day's labor. All, did I say? No; one solitary individual forms an exception. Bent, apparently, under the weight of some great sorrow, and leaning upon a staff, clad in the garb of a pilgrim, he moves silently onward. Follow him; your curiosity is justifiable, for he may interest you. Pass with him through the narrow streets, cross yonder bridge, enter that small church, through the doorway of which he passes. Behold! He kneels, his eyes are riveted upon some object. Approach nearer. Two marble slabs attract your attention. What means the inscription in Greek? On the one to the left I read Eiréné, on the other, the following sentences:

"Here lies all that is mortal of Dimitrios Phocas, who fell in 1480, at the siege of Rhodes, bravely fighting in defence of the faith. May he rest in peace!"

A little below I read as follows:

"The bodies of Dimitrios Phocas and Irene Diogenes which lie here awaiting the Resurrection were brought from Rhodes by the care of Vincent Morosini and his wife Helena, the sister of Dimitrios."

The pilgrim is deeply touched. The pallor of the

grave spreads over his face, he raises his hands, he speaks:

"My God, I have found them! My long life of penance is at an end. Soul of Dimitrios, soul of Irene, pardon me from the bosom of eternity. My God, I thank thee, let me now depart in peace."

Lo! the man falls forward upon the cold marble stones, he is motionless. Approach him, lay your hand upon his shoulders, you are touching a corpse.

*   *   *   *   *   *   *

The body of the pilgrim was found by the sacristan, and in his bosom lay concealed a paper containing the following:

"Over seas and lands have I wandered, since, almost miraculously, I was rescued from the waves, on that awful night. Long has been my penance, bitter were my tears, but a God of mercy has been merciful to me. I found rest for my soul in the bosom of the true faith on the tomb of Our Saviour at Jerusalem. Now, I seek for naught save to discover those whom I have injured, and to implore their pardon."

Morosini and Helena, having heard of this sudden death in the Church, defrayed the expenses of the funeral. The dead man was consigned to the earth at the feet of the two whose enemy he had been. A simple slab marks the place where he rests, bearing the single inscription: *"Nicolaus,"* the name of the one who there awaits the Resurrection together with the ashes of

DIMITRIOS AND IRENE.

DIMITRIOS AND IRENE

◁A Historical Romance,▷

BY

CHARLES WARREN CURRIER

Author of "Carmel in America," "History of Religious Orders," Etc.

ILLUSTRATED.

12mo. Cloth, 254 Pages.   Price, $1.00.

Gallery & McCann,

5 W. Mulberry St., Baltimore, Md.

CARDINAL'S RESIDENCE,
    408 N. Charles St., Baltimore.
        MARCH 15, 1894.

MY DEAR FATHER CURRIER:

I have to thank you for the copy of the historical romance, "DIMITRIOS AND IRENE," which you sent me.

The subject which you have chosen is rich in historical interest and gives ample scope in the field of fancy.

I hope you have been as successful in your new role, as you have been in the graver pursuits of historical research and sacred eloquence, and I am certain that your romance, whatever may be the success of the plot, will not offend the moral sense of the reader.

          Faithfully Yours, in Xt.,
                J. CARD. GIBBONS.

    201 I STREET, N. W., WASHINGTON, D. C.
            MARCH 21, 1894.

REV. CHARLES WARREN CURRIER:

REV. AND DEAR SIR:—I beg to acknowledge the receipt

irresistable in every line of "Dimitrios and Irene."—THE ORPHAN'S BOUQUET, Boston.

"Books should to one of these four ends conduce: For wisdom, piety, delight or use," says the poet. "Dimitrios and Irene; or, the Conquest of Constantinople," by the Rev. Charles Warren Currier, poesesses all these qualities marked out by the poet. The name of Father Currier, the author of "Carmel in America," needs no recommendation. He does honor to pen or pulpit.—CARMELITE REVIEW.

"Dimitrois and Irene; or, the conquest of Constantinople," is a historical romance of the fall of the city on the Bosphorous, and covers in a different manner nearly the same ground as the recent romance of Gen. Lew. Wallace. It is very well written, and the period is always picturesque and interesting.—BALTIMORE SUN.

Rich in information as General Wallace's book is on the topography and condition of Byzantium in pre-Turkish times, that of Father Currier is a treasury. As such, it must be eminently helpful to every one who desires some reliable knowledge of a period and a people of the most picturesque portion of the world, on a stage where so many gorgeous chapters of ancient history were enacted.—CATHOLIC WORLD.

The story, which is fascinating from beginning to end, is evidently the fruit of deep study. The style is brilliant, and the characters well drawn.—DONAHOE'S MAGAZINE.

The author is, evidently, master of his subject. Besides, his plot is skilfully managed, his language choice and appropriate, and the work abounds in pathetic passages and vivid descriptions. God speed the book and grant us many more like it.—THE ANNALS OF OUR LADY OF THE SACRED HEART.

www.ingramcontent.com/pod-product-compliance
Lightning Source LLC
Chambersburg PA
CBHW020756230426
43666CB00007B/727